MARY
Makes it Easy

BBC Books, an imprint of Ebury Publishing
20 Vauxhall Bridge Road,
London SW1V 2SA

BBC Books is part of the Penguin Random House group of companies
whose addresses can be found at global.penguinrandomhouse.com

Photography by Laura Edwards
Cover Photography by Nicky Johnston

First published by BBC Books in 2023

www.penguin.co.uk

A CIP catalogue record for this book is available from the British Library

ISBN 9781785948428

Publishing Director: Lizzy Gray
Editor: Phoebe Lindsley
Project Editor and Copyeditor: Jo Roberts-Miller
Food Stylist: Lisa Harrison
Prop Stylist: Tabitha Hawkins
Food Stylist Assistants: Jess McIntosh, Ellie Fleming
Design: Hart Studio

Colour origination by Altaimage, London

Printed and bound in Germany by Mohn Media Mohndruck GmbH

Penguin Random House is committed to a sustainable future for
our business, our readers and our planet. This book is made
from Forest Stewardship Council® certified paper.

MARY
Makes it Easy

The new ultimate stress-free cookbook

Contents

Introduction

As a home cook, I understand the challenges that can come with preparing delicious meals day after day, especially when juggling a busy schedule. In our frantic modern lives, we have many things that take up time and cause us stress, and I believe that cooking and preparing food for friends and family shouldn't be one of them. Over the years I have learnt many tips and tricks to make cooking at home as easy as possible, and I am delighted to share these with you now.

The key to making cooking easy is being prepared. Before starting to cook, make sure that you have read the recipe thoroughly and checked your cupboards to see what you already have, before making a list of what you need to buy. By getting everything prepared beforehand – all the ingredients out and measured, the oven heating and the right pans or trays out – you'll find it much easier when it comes to working through the steps of the recipe. I tend to write the measurements on the bottom of trays and tins with a marker pen to see their size and capacity at a glance, making sure I always have the right sized tin for the job. I don't bother with lots of fancy tins that you don't use, but rather have a small selection of regular-sized trays and cookware that I like to use again and again.

Throughout this book you will find small icons indicating some 'easy' qualities a recipe has – for instance whether it can be prepared in advance, cooked in just one pot or roasting tin or frozen easily. You can see at a glance how to fit the recipes into your busy lives and plan your meals accordingly – whether you are cooking for one or many!

I find the freezer can be a wonderful asset in the kitchen, so we have created a Grown-up Chocolate Birthday Cake (p214) that can be baked in a rectangular roasting tray and freezes excellently. A little goes a long way – I have one in my freezer now, which we take slices off with a hot knife whenever we need a treat. Just make sure when cooking from the freezer that you leave enough time for things to defrost.

Whilst making everything from scratch is ideal, when you're busy you sometimes need to take a few shortcuts here and there. In the recipes that follow you will find pre-bought jars of hollandaise or lemon curd. I always buy pre-made puff pastry as I find I never have the time to make it from scratch at home, and bought puff pastry is first class. Equally, preparing things in advance will always save you time when you are in a rush. I have a tin of the Somerset Cheddar Cheese Straws (p31) on the side of my kitchen, ready to enjoy with a bowl of soup for a quick lunch or alongside a drink with friends.

I have also tried to include recipes within this book to make hosting as simple as possible, to give you more time to enjoy with your guests. We have included lots of simple canapés to prepare ahead of time, instead of a traditional first course, so that all you need to do on the day is prepare a main meal. You could host an easy, but impressive, dinner party by having the light, summery Gazpacho (p25) or the elegant Sweet Chilli Prawn Canapés (p21), followed by the Easy Peasy One-pot Chicken (p79) or the Lemon and Caper Salmon Linguine (p56). For an incredibly easy dessert I would choose the Express Apple and Pear Open Pie (p275) with its glorious lemon curd centre, and you can never go wrong with a pavlova (p251).

Do make sure that you are tasting as you go along, and if you feel you need to add or remove anything from the recipes to suit your taste – make sure you do! There is nothing worse than sitting down to a meal and having your first mouthful, only to find it needs some more pepper or sweetening with redcurrant jelly, so taste, test and add along the way.

Making mistakes is part of cooking. I find I make mistakes all the time, so be kind to yourself and use the tips and tricks throughout this book to help make things run as smoothly as possible. From quick and easy weeknight dinners to showstopping desserts, each recipe in this book has been carefully tested, with fewer ingredients and more detailed explanations, to ensure stress-free home cooking.

Whether you're looking to impress with a special dinner or simply want to put a comforting meal on the table after a long day, this book will make it easier for you to get into the kitchen and create something delicious for yourself as well as your family and friends.

Mary Berry

Cook's Notes to Make Life Easy in the Kitchen

Here are a few notes to help you in the kitchen for a stress-free life. With a few basic steps and tips, cooking can be easy and simple to do.

Before you start

Read the recipe all the way through before cooking. That way, you'll have a clear idea of the steps you need to take. Check that you have all the correct equipment – the right sized tin, for example – and that your oven is set to the right temperature and all the ingredients are weighed accurately. This is so important. I suggest using digital scales for accuracy. Now, you are set to go!

Oven temperatures

As ovens vary in the amount of heat they produce, you may need to cook a dish for slightly longer or shorter than the recipe stipulates, depending on your oven. It can be helpful to use an oven thermometer to find out how accurate your oven is.

Metric and imperial

I have provided both metric and imperial measurements. When you are following a recipe, it's best to stick to one or the other – particularly if you are baking. (See also the Conversion Chart on pages 280–1.) Spoon measurements are level measuring spoons, unless otherwise stated.

Tins and equipment

Try to use the size of tins and dishes I suggest, otherwise the food can cook differently. If your roasting tin, for example, is slightly larger than I recommend, the liquid may evaporate more quickly and the sauce may be too thick. Similarly, if your tin is smaller, it will cook more slowly and the sauce may be too runny.

Ovenproof frying pans and flameproof casseroles

A number of the savoury stews and one-pan dishes I have included in this book begin on the hob and end up in the oven. I tend to use large, deep frying pans, as the ones I have at home are ovenproof, but it would be just as good to use a flameproof casserole dish. So long as it has a lid that fits and is suitable to use on the hob and in the oven, it will do the job.

Eggs

Use large eggs, unless otherwise stated – free-range, if possible.

Seasoning

Adding salt and pepper is a very important part of cooking. Seasoning brings out the flavour of the ingredients and I season each part of the recipe as I go along. Taste before serving, to check.

Sustainable fish

We must protect our oceans so buy fish that is sustainably sourced – this means it has been fished in such a way that doesn't damage fish stocks by over-fishing and protects the habitat. It will advertise itself as such on the packet, or ask your fishmonger or at the fish counter in your local supermarket. The levels of fish stocks do change, so while I have tried to include fish that are on the sustainability list, do swap one for another if necessary.

Vegetarian and vegan recipes

More and more often, I will choose to cook without meat when I'm at home. I have included a wide variety of vegetarian dishes here – starters, main courses and even a vegan dessert, the Sunset Fruit Platter (p257).

Melting chocolate

Melting chocolate in a microwave can be a quick and convenient way to do it, but be careful not to overheat. Just make sure you heat the chocolate in 20–30 second bursts and take it out of the microwave to stir regularly. I also like to melt chocolate in a small heatproof bowl over a pan of just simmering water, as it gives a lovely shiny finish. White chocolate only needs to be warm (not hot) to melt. If it gets too hot it will not set again when cold or chilled.

Recipe icons

In our hope to make these recipes as easy to follow as possible, we've added an icon to show you at a glance which of these six 'easy' qualities each recipe has. Often a recipe will have more than one easy feature, but we've picked the quality we think is most helpful.

 ONE POT

 5 INGREDIENTS OR FEWER

 PREP AHEAD

 QUICK COOK

 FREEZES WELL

 FOR A CROWD

Light Bites
and Canapés

Cucumber and Crab Bites 16

Smoked Salmon Canapé Sandwiches 19

Sweet Chilli Prawn Canapés 21

Grilled Lemon Edamame Beans 22

Gazpacho 25

Smart Chestnut Mushroom Soup 26

Thai Green Chicken Noodle Soup 28

Somerset Cheddar Cheese Straws 31

Dolcelatte and Sage Scone Canapés 32

Classic Basil Pesto Dip 34

Soured Cream and Chive Dip 34

Hummus Dip 37

Guacamole 37

Sausage Nuggets with Red Pepper Sauce 38

Watermelon, Feta and Parma Ham 41

Three Flavoured Butters 42

Crayfish and Avocado Cocktail 45

Fabulous Fish Sharing Platter 47

Cucumber and Crab Bites

These little bites are great at a party – they're simple and look impressive. Make and serve on the same day.

Makes about 20

2 tbsp full-fat cream cheese

3 tbsp small capers
    from a jar, drained

1 tsp lemon juice

¼ red chilli, finely diced

1 tbsp chopped chives

115g (4oz) fresh white
    crabmeat, drained
    of excess liquid

A few drops of Tabasco

1 thin cucumber, peeled
    and sliced into 1–1.5cm
    (½in) rounds

Freshly chopped
    parsley, to serve

Mary's Tips

*Can be assembled up
to 6 hours ahead.*

Not suitable for freezing.

1. Measure the cream cheese into a bowl. Add half the capers, the lemon juice, half the chilli and all the chives and mix well.

2. Stir the crabmeat and Tabasco into the mixture and season well with salt and freshly ground black pepper.

3. Stamp out the seeds of each slice of cucumber using a small piping nozzle or small cutter to make a ring, or carefully run a small pointed knife around the seeds and lift out.

4. Spoon some of the topping into each ring. Arrange a few of the remaining capers, some diced chilli and a little parsley on each bite and place on a long platter to serve.

 FOR A CROWD

Smoked Salmon Canapé Sandwiches

A favourite sandwich, now bite-size. Simple to make and they look particularly lovely when presented on their sides, as they are here.

Makes 24

1 small loaf brown bread, unsliced

175g (6oz) full-fat cream cheese

200g (7oz) smoked salmon slices

A few sprigs of fresh dill, chopped

Juice of ½ lemon

Mary's Tips

Can be made up to 8 hours ahead; cover in lightly damp kitchen towel and cling film or eco wrap to keep fresh.

Not suitable for freezing.

1. Remove the crusts from the loaf and cut the loaf into 12 very thin slices (you may not need the whole loaf). If the bread is very fresh, wrap it in foil and freeze until firm before slicing – about 2 hours.

2. Place 4 slices of bread on a board. Spread one side of each slice with cream cheese. Top with half the smoked salmon slices and sprinkle with some of the dill.

3. Place another 4 slices of bread on the board. Spread cream cheese on both sides of these slices, then rest them on top of the salmon. Top with the remaining salmon slices, then sprinkle with some more dill.

4. Take the final 4 slices of bread and spread cream cheese on one side. Place the bread cream-cheese-side down on top of the salmon and press firmly. You will have 4 sandwiches with 3 layers of bread and 2 layers of salmon.

5. Slice 6 small rectangles out of each sandwich, then turn them on their sides, so the filling is visible on top. Arrange the 24 little sandwiches on a platter.

6. Squeeze a little lemon juice over the top before serving.

 FOR A CROWD

Sweet Chilli Prawn Canapés

With a crispy base and a Japanese-inspired filling, these are an easy and impressive canapé, perfect to go with drinks at a party.

Makes 12

3 slices white bread
   from a large tin loaf
30g (1oz) butter, melted
1 garlic clove, finely grated

Prawn Filling
½ tsp white miso paste
1 tbsp sweet chilli sauce
1 tsp rice wine vinegar
1 tsp soy sauce
½ tsp finely grated
   fresh root ginger
1 tbsp sunflower or sesame oil
2 spring onions, trimmed
   and finely sliced
2 tbsp freshly chopped
   parsley
175g (6oz) small cooked
   North Atlantic prawns

Mary's Tips

The cases can be cooked up to a day ahead. Fill with prawns up to 2 hours ahead.

Not suitable for freezing.

1. Preheat the oven to 200°C/Fan 180°C/Gas 6. You will need a 12-hole mini-muffin tin.

2. Place the bread on a work surface. Roll the slices out very thinly, using a rolling pin, until they are each about 12.5cm (5in) square. Use a bread knife to remove the crusts and cut each slice into 4 squares.

3. Mix the melted butter and garlic together in a small bowl. Brush both sides of the bread squares, then use them to line the holes of the mini muffin tin. Press down firmly into the holes. Bake in the preheated oven for about 8–10 minutes, until golden and crisp. Keep an eye on them, as they darken quickly. Set aside to cool in the tin.

4. Meanwhile, make the prawn filling. Mix the miso, sweet chilli sauce, rice wine vinegar, soy, ginger and oil together in a small bowl. Add the spring onions and parsley and mix well.

5. Drain the prawns of any water and dry very well on kitchen paper. Add them to the bowl, season with freshly ground black pepper and stir well.

6. Spoon the filling into the cases to serve.

FOR A CROWD

Grilled Lemon Edamame Beans

Sometimes the simplest of recipes are the tastiest. These are perfect as a snack instead of processed crisps. If you cannot buy fresh beans, the frozen ones are good, too. These are best eaten with fingers, so you may wish to serve finger-washing bowls, too!

Makes a large bowlful

500g (1lb 2oz) edamame
    beans in their pods
3 tbsp olive oil
Juice of ½ lemon

Mary's Tips

Best made and served.

Not suitable for freezing.

1. Preheat the grill to high.

2. Bring a large pan of water to the boil. Once boiling, add the beans and cook for 3 minutes. (If using frozen beans, wait until the water has come back to the boil before timing 3 minutes.) Drain and refresh in cold water. Set aside to dry.

3. Tip the dry beans into a large shallow roasting tin. Drizzle over the oil and toss to coat. Arrange the beans in a single layer in the tin and place under the preheated grill for 5 minutes, turning over after the pods are tinged brown.

4. Remove the beans from the grill, drizzle with the lemon juice and season well with sea salt.

5. Pile into a bowl and serve hot.

 QUICK COOK

Gazpacho

A classic cold soup made from raw summer vegetables. This traditional dish originates from the Andalusian region of Spain where it is served cold due to the hot summer climate. To skin the tomatoes, make a cross with a small knife on the stalk end, then plunge into boiling water for about 50 seconds to loosen the skin. Transfer them to cold water and the skin should come away easily.

Serves 6

55g (2oz) white sourdough bread, crusts removed

1kg (2lb 4oz) medium very ripe tomatoes, skinned

½ large cucumber, peeled, deseeded and roughly chopped

1 small garlic clove, finely grated

1 red pepper, deseeded and roughly chopped

1 medium banana shallot, roughly chopped

4 tbsp extra-virgin olive oil, plus extra for drizzling

2 tbsp white wine vinegar

1 tbsp tomato purée

½ tsp sugar

To Garnish

1 tomato, deseeded and very finely chopped

¼ cucumber, peeled, deseeded and very finely chopped

¼ red pepper, deseeded and very finely chopped

Mary's Tips

Can be made up to 2 days ahead.

1. Tear the bread into pieces and place in a bowl. Add 150ml (¼ pint) water and leave to soak for 10 minutes.

2. Cut each tomato in half, discard the hard central stem, keeping the seeds, and slice the tomatoes into quarters.

3. Place the tomatoes, cucumber, garlic, pepper, shallot, oil, vinegar, tomato purée and sugar into the bowl with the bread. Season well with salt and freshly ground black pepper. Whiz with an electric hand blender or food processor until smooth.

4. Pour the soup into a jug and chill in the fridge for 1 hour.

5. Spoon the gazpacho into bowls, drizzle with olive oil and garnish with the chopped vegetables. Serve well chilled.

 FREEZES WELL

Smart Chestnut Mushroom Soup

This soup is fairly rich and feels quite extravagant. Chestnut mushrooms, also known as brown mushrooms, have a firm texture and earthy flavour. They are my favourite for a soup or sauce, as they have more flavour than button mushrooms.

Serves 4–6

55g (2oz) butter

1 tbsp sunflower oil

2 onions, finely chopped

2 celery sticks, diced

1 garlic clove, finely grated

1kg (2lb 4oz) chestnut mushrooms, sliced

700ml (1¼ pints) chicken or vegetable stock

2 tbsp soy sauce

150ml (¼ pint) pouring double cream

3 tbsp freshly chopped parsley

Mary's Tips

Can be made up to 2 days ahead.

1. Melt the butter and oil in a large saucepan over a high heat. Add the onions and celery and cook for 5 minutes, then stir in the garlic and fry for 30 seconds.

2. Add the mushrooms to the saucepan and fry for about 5 minutes, until golden but not wet, turning them regularly.

3. Pour in the stock and bring up to the boil. Reduce the heat, cover with a lid and simmer for about 20 minutes, or until the vegetables are tender.

4. Ladle into a food processor or blender and whiz until smooth.

5. Return the soup to the saucepan over a medium heat and stir in the soy sauce and most of the cream. Season to taste with salt and freshly ground black pepper, then serve in warm soup bowls. Drizzle with the remaining cream and scatter the parsley over the top.

 FREEZES WELL

Thai Green Chicken Noodle Soup

A meal in a bowl, this warming soup is bursting with aromatic flavours. It's also a good recipe for using leftover cooked chicken from a roast. You could use thighs instead of breasts, if you prefer.

Serves 6

2 litres (3½ pints) good chicken stock

250g (9oz) skinless boneless chicken breasts

2 large banana shallots, thinly sliced

2 garlic cloves, finely grated

1 tbsp finely grated fresh root ginger

½ red chilli, deseeded and finely chopped

1–2 tbsp Thai green curry paste

2 tsp fish sauce

1 tsp light muscovado sugar

115g (4oz) button mushrooms, sliced

2 small pak choi, sliced into large pieces

½ bunch of coriander, leaves chopped

Juice of 1 lime

2 nests 100g (3½oz) fine egg noodles

1. Place the chicken breasts and stock in a large saucepan. Bring up to the boil, then reduce the heat and simmer very gently for about 15 minutes until the chicken is cooked through. Remove the chicken with a slotted spoon, then chop into pieces and set aside.

2. Add the shallots, garlic, ginger, chilli, curry paste, fish sauce, sugar and mushrooms to the poaching stock and simmer for 5 minutes over a medium heat.

3. Add the pak choi, coriander and cooked chicken to the pan and simmer for a final 3 minutes. Stir in the lime juice and season to taste with salt and freshly ground black pepper.

4. Just before serving, cook the noodle nests in a pan of boiling water according to the packet instructions. Drain and divide the noodles between 6 soup bowls. Ladle the hot soup over the top to serve.

Mary's Tips

Soup base can be made up to 8 hours ahead. Add the noodles to serve.

Not suitable for freezing.

 PREP AHEAD

Somerset Cheddar Cheese Straws

Cheese straws are so delicious but can be tricky to make if the proportions are not quite right. We tested these every week for a month, just to make sure they were perfect – and because they are so moreish, too!

Makes 50

250g (9oz) cold butter, cubed
55g (2oz) semolina
400g (14oz) plain flour
1 tsp mustard powder
¼ tsp cayenne pepper
150g (5oz) mature Somerset Cheddar, coarsely grated
150g (5oz) Parmesan, coarsely grated, plus about 4 tbsp finely grated, to garnish
1 egg, beaten
A little milk

Mary's Tips

Store in an airtight tin for up to 3 weeks

Before serving, reheat in a moderate oven for about 5 minutes, cool then serve.

1. Preheat the oven to 200°C/Fan 180°C/Gas 6. Line 2 large baking sheets with non-stick baking paper.

2. Measure the butter, semolina, flour, mustard powder, cayenne pepper and a little salt into a food processor. Whiz until the mixture looks like breadcrumbs.

3. Add the Cheddar, Parmesan and egg and whiz again for a short time, just until the dough comes together.

4. Remove the dough from the processor, divide into two equal pieces, and shape each one with your hands on a floured work surface into a rectangle. Roll each piece of dough to a rectangle about 46 x 16cm (18 × 6½in) and about 8mm (⅓in) thick.

5. Brush the milk over the top of the dough and sprinkle with the finely grated Parmesan. Slice each rectangle into roughly 25 strips.

6. Carefully lift each straw on to the prepared baking sheets and bake in the preheated oven for about 18 minutes, or until golden brown. Leave to cool on the baking sheet until the straws have hardened and are easy to handle.

7. Serve cold.

 FREEZES WELL

Dolcelatte and Sage Scone Canapés

*Tiny bite-sized herb and cheese scones, these are topped with
Dolcelatte. Don't handle the dough too much or it will become tough.
If you can't find Dolcelatte, you could use Stilton instead.*

Makes about 70

125g (4½oz) self-raising flour
½ tsp baking powder
30g (1oz) butter,
    softened and cubed
55g (2oz) Parmesan,
    finely grated
1 tsp mustard powder
1 tbsp finely chopped
    fresh sage
1 egg, beaten
2 tbsp milk, plus
    extra to glaze
150g (5oz) Dolcelatte cheese
2 tsp cranberry sauce
Small bunch of flat-
    leaf parsley, leaves
    picked, to garnish

Mary's Tips

*Scones can be made a day ahead.
Assemble up to 4 hours ahead
and pop in oven for the cheese
to melt, just before serving.*

Scones freeze well.

1. Preheat the oven to 200°C/Fan 180°C/Gas 6 and line
a baking sheet with non-stick baking paper.

2. Measure the flour, baking powder and butter into a bowl.
Rub in the butter using your fingertips until the mixture looks
like breadcrumbs.

3. Stir in the Parmesan, mustard powder and sage, and season
with salt and freshly ground black pepper.

4. Place the beaten egg in a bowl or jug and add the milk.
Pour into the flour mixture and bring together with your
hands, adding a dash more milk, if needed, to make a soft
dough. Gently knead, then roll out on a floured work surface
to about 1–2cm (½–¾in) thick. Cut out rounds using a 3cm
(1¼in) cutter, re-rolling to cut more. You should get about
35 mini scones.

5. Place the scones on the prepared baking sheet and brush
the tops with a little milk. Bake in the preheated oven for
about 8 minutes, until pale golden and risen. Remove from
the oven and leave to cool on a wire rack.

6. Slice each scone in half widthways and return to the baking
sheet. Spread a little Dolcelatte on top of each half and return
to the oven for about 2–3 minutes to melt slightly.

7. Top each half with a small blob of cranberry sauce and
a tiny parsley leaf, and serve warm.

 FOR A CROWD

Classic Basil Pesto Dip

Blanching the basil helps to keep the bright green colour. Serve with a selection of prepared vegetables for dipping.

Makes 525g (1lb 3oz)

150g (5oz) fresh basil, including stalks
115g (4oz) pine nuts
115g (4oz) Parmesan, grated
3 large garlic cloves, finely grated
150ml (¼ pint) olive oil
Juice of ½ lemon
½ tsp caster sugar

<u>Mary's Tips</u>

Can be made up to 4 days ahead.

Not suitable for freezing.

1. Bring a large saucepan of water to the boil. Add the basil leaves and stalks and blanch for 15 seconds. Drain and run under cold water. Squeeze out any water and dry on kitchen paper.

2. Toast the pine nuts in a small non-stick frying pan over a medium heat, gently turning until golden. Set aside to cool.

3. Put all the ingredients into a small food processor and whiz until you have a dipping consistency. Season with salt and freshly ground pepper to taste.

4. Serve with strips of pepper, carrot, radishes, cauliflower florets or leaves of red chicory.

 QUICK COOK

Soured Cream and Chive Dip

So, so simple to make, and much better than shop-bought varieties. Serve with toasted pitta bread and crunchy vegetables.

Makes 300g (10½oz)

300g (10½oz) soured cream
Small bunch of chives, snipped
1 tsp lemon juice

<u>Mary's Tips</u>

Can be made up to 4 days ahead.

Not suitable for freezing.

1. Measure all the ingredients into a bowl. Season with salt and freshly ground black pepper and mix well.

 QUICK COOK

Hummus Dip

A very popular dip to serve with pitta bread, crackers and crudités.
It is also good added to the Nourish Bowls on page 158.

Makes 400g (14oz)

1 × 400g tin chickpeas,
  drained and rinsed
1 garlic clove, finely grated
Juice of 1 large lemon
8 tbsp olive oil, plus
  extra for drizzling
2 tbsp natural yoghurt
1 tsp ground cumin

Mary's Tips

Not suitable for freezing.

Can be made up to 2 days ahead.

1. Add all the ingredients to a food processor and season with salt and freshly ground black pepper. Whiz until smooth.

2. Serve in a bowl with a little olive oil drizzled on top.

 QUICK COOK

Guacamole

Delicious as a dip, on toast or served with the Mixed
Bean and Red Pepper Chilli on page 147.

Serves 4–6

2 small ripe avocados,
  peeled and diced
1 medium tomato,
  deseeded and chopped
½ garlic clove, finely grated
½ small onion, finely chopped
Juice of 1 large lime
2 tbsp olive oil
½ bunch of coriander,
  leaves roughly chopped
A few drops of Tabasco

Mary's Tips

Can be made up to an hour ahead.

Not suitable for freezing.

1. Place all the ingredients in a bowl and season well with salt and freshly ground black pepper. Mix together, mashing with the back of a fork to achieve a chunky consistency.

2. Serve cold in a pretty bowl.

 QUICK COOK

Sausage Nuggets with Red Pepper Sauce

Great as a hot canapé, to serve instead of a starter, or as a light lunch.

Makes 40

6 good pork sausages

½ small red onion,
cut into wedges

55g (2oz) cracker
biscuits, crushed

1 tbsp freshly chopped
parsley

2 tsp grainy mustard

55g (2oz) roasted red
peppers from a jar, diced

55g (2oz) mature
Cheddar, grated

30g (1oz) plain flour

2 tbsp sunflower oil

Red Pepper Sauce

1 tbsp olive oil

2 large shallots, finely sliced

1 garlic clove, finely grated

200g (7oz) roasted red
peppers from a jar,
roughly chopped

½ x 400g tin chopped
tomatoes

1 tbsp tomato purée

½ tsp caster sugar

1 tbsp freshly chopped
parsley

1. To make the red pepper sauce, heat the oil in a large saucepan over a medium heat. Add the shallots and fry for 2–3 minutes. Stir in the garlic and peppers and fry for a few more minutes. Add the chopped tomatoes, tomato purée, sugar and parsley, and pour in 100ml (3½fl oz) water, mix well, cover with a lid and bring up to the boil. Reduce the heat and simmer for about 15 minutes. Remove from the heat and blitz until smooth in a food processor or with an electric hand blender.

2. Meanwhile, remove the skin from the sausages and place in a food processor. Add the onion wedges, crackers, parsley, mustard, peppers and Cheddar. Season well with salt and freshly ground black pepper and whiz until the mixture is finely chopped. Shape into 40 small round nuggets and roll in the plain flour to coat.

3. Heat the sunflower oil in a large frying pan over a medium heat. Add the nuggets and cook for 8–10 minutes, turning until lightly golden and cooked through (you may need to do this in batches).

4. Serve the hot nuggets on a platter with a bowl of the red pepper sauce.

Mary's Tips

Nuggets can be made up to 8 hours ahead. Sauce can be made up to a day ahead.

Nuggets freeze well uncooked. Sauce freezes well.

 FOR A CROWD

Watermelon, Feta and Parma Ham

Super easy and a delicious canapé or party platter. The saltiness of the Parma ham, creaminess of the feta and freshness of the watermelon are the perfect combination.

Makes 24

6 slices Parma ham
115g (4oz) feta cheese, cut into 24 cubes
24 mint leaves
150g (5oz) watermelon, cut into 24 cubes

You will need 24 cocktail sticks.

Mary's Tips

Can be assembled up to 4 hours ahead.

Not suitable for freezing.

1. You will need 24 cocktail sticks.

2. Cut each slice of Parma ham into 4 and roll up into a neat tube.

3. Using a cocktail stick, spear a cube of feta, then a mint leaf, then a cube of watermelon and finally a roll of Parma ham. Repeat with the remaining ingredients.

4. Chill until needed and serve at room temperature.

5 INGREDIENTS OR FEWER

Three Flavoured Butters

Keep these butters in the fridge to use on top of grilled meats or fish. The Branston Pickle butter would be wonderful on top of a jacket potato at lunchtime.

**Enough for
6 steaks or 4
baked potatoes**

Black Olive Butter
75g (3oz) butter, softened
5 pitted black olives,
    finely chopped

Chilli and Garlic Butter
75g (3oz) butter, softened
½ red chilli, finely chopped
1 large garlic clove,
    finely grated

Branston Pickle Butter
75g (3oz) butter, softened
1 tbsp Branston Pickle

Mary's Tips

Can be wrapped in cling film or eco wrap and kept in the fridge for up to 2 weeks.

Freeze well for up to 3 months.

Black Olive Butter

1. Put the butter, olives and some salt and freshly ground black pepper in a mixing bowl. Beat well.

2. Place the olive butter on a piece of cling film or eco wrap and roll into a log shape about the thickness of a £1 coin. Wrap tightly and chill in the fridge for 1 hour, or until firm.

3. Slice into rounds to serve.

Chilli and Garlic Butter

1. Place the butter, chilli, garlic and some salt and freshly ground black pepper in a mixing bowl. Beat well.

2. Place the chilli and garlic butter on a piece of cling film or eco wrap and roll into a log shape about the thickness of a £1 coin. Wrap tightly and chill in the fridge for 1 hour, or until firm.

3. Slice into rounds to serve.

Branston Pickle Butter

1. Place the butter, pickle and some salt and freshly ground black pepper in a mixing bowl. Beat well.

2. Place the Branston Pickle butter on a piece of cling film or eco wrap and roll into a log shape about the thickness of a £1 coin. Wrap tightly and chill in the fridge for 1 hour, or until firm.

3. Slice into rounds to serve.

 FREEZES WELL

Crayfish and Avocado Cocktail

One of my favourite light lunches or first courses. Replace the crayfish with prawns or crab, if preferred, or if you can't find crayfish. They are readily available in fishmongers and all good supermarkets at certain times of year.

Serves 4

225g (8oz) cooked
  shelled crayfish tails
1 large avocado, peeled
  and quartered
2 Little Gem lettuces,
  shredded
4 thin slices lemon, to garnish

Cocktail Sauce

3 tbsp crème fraîche
4 tbsp mayonnaise
1 tbsp sun-dried tomato paste
1 tbsp hot horseradish sauce
A few drops of
  Worcestershire sauce
A few drops of Tabasco
Squeeze of fresh lemon juice
2 tbsp tomato ketchup
2 tbsp freshly chopped
  dill, plus 4 tiny
  sprigs, to garnish

Mary's Tips

*Can be assembled up
to an hour ahead.*

Not suitable for freezing.

1. Set aside 4 crayfish tails for decoration.

2. To make the cocktail sauce, mix all the ingredients in a bowl and season with salt and freshly ground pepper.

3. Pat the crayfish tails dry using kitchen paper and add to the sauce.

4. Dice three-quarters of the avocado and thinly slice the remaining quarter. Add the diced avocado to the sauce and crayfish mix well.

5. Divide the shredded lettuce between 4 glasses and spoon the crayfish mixture on top.

6. Arrange the reserved crayfish tails on the surface of each cocktail, alongside a few slices of avocado, a slice of lemon and a sprig of dill.

 QUICK COOK

Fabulous Fish Sharing Platter

For lunch or supper, this is such a treat. So simple and all about the presentation. Smoked trout will be just as delicious as smoked salmon, if you would prefer. Leaving the shell on some of the quail eggs looks really pretty.

Serves 6

150g (5oz) cooked tiger
    or king prawns

12 quail eggs, hard boiled and
    6 peeled and 6 half-peeled

1 tsp celery salt

2 Little Gem lettuces,
    cut into wedges

150g (5oz) hot-smoked
    salmon fillet, broken
    into pieces

200g (7oz) smoked
    salmon slices

1 jar dill pickle

1 large lemon, sliced
    into 6 wedges

1 tbsp freshly snipped chives

4–6 slices rye bread, to serve

Lemon Chive Dressing

6 tbsp mayonnaise

4 tbsp crème fraîche

Juice of ½ large lemon

1 tbsp freshly snipped chives

1 tbsp hot horseradish sauce

Mary's Tips

*Dressing can be made up
to 3 days ahead.*

*Assemble up to 3 hours
ahead and keep chilled.*

Not suitable for freezing.

1. To make the lemon chive dressing, measure all the ingredients into a small bowl. Mix well and season with salt and freshly ground black pepper. Set aside 3 tablespoons, then add the king prawns to the bowl with the remaining dressing and mix well.

2. Place two small serving bowls onto a wooden board. Put the prawns in one bowl and the quail eggs in another. Sprinkle the eggs with the celery salt.

3. Arrange the Little Gem wedges on the board. Place the hot-smoked salmon and smoked salmon slices around the bowls, and put the jar of pickle on the board. Place the lemon wedges by the salmon and scatter the chives on top.

4. Drizzle the reserved lemon and chive dressing over the lettuce wedges just before serving, with the slices of rye bread on the side.

 FOR A CROWD

Fish

Salmon and Herbed Hollandaise Pavé

*These are mini versions of a salmon en croûte. There can often
be too much pastry with en croûte. Use the puff pastry in a single
layer; there will be some pastry left over. Choose thin salmon fillets
that are all the same shape and size, so they cook evenly.*

Serves 4

1 × 325g packet ready-rolled
all-butter puff pastry

4 x 125g (4½oz) salmon
fillets, skinned

1 tsp paprika

Herbed Hollandaise

8 tbsp hollandaise
sauce from a jar

4 tsp freshly chopped
tarragon

4 tsp freshly chopped basil

Zest of 1 lemon

Mary's Tips

*Sauce can be made up to
2 days ahead (the flavours
will get stronger with age).
Assemble the salmon on the
pastry up to 6 hours ahead.*

Not suitable for freezing.

1. Preheat the oven to 200°C/Fan 180°C/Gas 6 and preheat
a large baking sheet.

2. To make the herbed hollandaise, measure all the ingredients
into a bowl and mix well. Season with salt and freshly ground
black pepper to taste.

3. Unroll the pastry. Slice the pastry into 4 rectangular strips,
slightly bigger than the salmon fillets.

4. Place the four rectangles of pastry onto a piece of non-stick
baking paper and prick the pastry all over with a fork.

5. Spread a teaspoon of the herbed hollandaise in the centre
of each rectangle, then sit a salmon fillet on top. Season well,
then spread a teaspoon of the sauce on top of each fillet.
Sprinkle with the paprika.

6. Carefully transfer the salmon and the non-stick baking
paper onto the hot baking sheet. Bake in the preheated oven
for about 18 minutes, or until the salmon is cooked and the
pastry is golden.

7. Using a fish slice, carefully slide each salmon and pastry
onto a plate or platter, and serve with green vegetables and
the remaining sauce in a bowl to pass around.

 PREP AHEAD

Cold Salmon Fillets
with Cucumber and Dill Sauce

For such a simple cold salmon dish, this is very easy and tasty. The sauce would be good with a whole poached salmon, too. This would be great for a party as part of a buffet table or sharing platter. Sprinkling the salt over the cucumber and onion draws out the excess liquid, which prevents the sauce from becoming too wet.

Serves 4

4 x 150g (5oz) salmon
   fillets, skin on
Large knob of butter
Juice of ½ lemon

Cucumber and
Dill Sauce

½ cucumber, peeled,
   deseeded and finely diced
½ red onion, finely chopped
1 tsp salt
Bunch of dill, stalks set aside
   and leaves chopped, plus
   4 small sprigs to garnish
100ml (3½fl oz)
   natural yoghurt
3 tbsp mayonnaise
1 tbsp white wine vinegar

Mary's Tips

Salmon can be cooked up to 8 hours ahead. Serve at room temperature. Sauce can be made up to 2 days ahead (the flavours will get stronger with age).

Not suitable for freezing.

1. Preheat the oven to 180°C/Fan 160°C/Gas 4.

2. To make the cucumber and dill sauce, place the cucumber and onion in a sieve and sprinkle with the salt. Mix well, then sit the sieve over a bowl and leave for 30 minutes until some of the liquid has drained. Rinse the cucumber and onion under cold water, then pat dry.

3. Place the cucumber and onion in a bowl. Add the dill, yoghurt, mayonnaise and vinegar and mix well. Season with freshly ground black pepper to taste.

4. Line a small roasting tin with a large piece of foil. Place the salmon fillets on the foil, skin-side down. Break the butter into four and put a knob on each fillet. Drizzle the lemon juice over the fish and season well. Scatter the dill stalks alongside, then fold the foil over the fish to make a parcel. Bake in the preheated oven for about 15 minutes, until just cooked. The salmon should be a flat pink colour all the way through. Take care not to overcook. Set aside to cool. Peel away the skin and discard.

5. Arrange the salmon on a plate, garnish with the reserved dill sprigs and serve with the sauce alongside.

 PREP AHEAD

Lemon and Caper Salmon Linguine

A super, quick, mid-week supper. The sharpness of the capers and lemon cuts through the creaminess of the salmon and pasta. Use tagliatelle, spaghetti or pappardelle, if preferred to linguine. Hot-smoked salmon is fresh salmon which has been lightly hot smoked, so the texture is more like cooked salmon than smoked salmon.

Serves 4

225g (8oz) linguine
75g (3oz) pine nuts
Small knob of butter
6 spring onions, trimmed
   and finely sliced
6 tbsp olive oil
Juice of 2 lemons
115g (4oz) capers from
   a jar, drained
Small bunch of
   chives, chopped
Small bunch of parsley,
   leaves chopped
200g (7oz) hot-smoked
   salmon flakes or fillets

Mary's Tips

Best made and served.

Not suitable for freezing.

1. Cook the pasta in boiling salted water according to the packet instructions. Drain, reserving 75ml (2½fl oz) of the pasta water.

2. Place a frying pan over a high heat. Add the pine nuts and cook for about 30 seconds until toasted and golden brown. Remove and set aside.

3. Add the butter and spring onions to the pan, and fry for about 30 seconds. Pour in the oil, lemon juice and capers and heat for a moment.

4. Add the cooked pasta, reserved pasta water, herbs and salmon. Season with salt and freshly ground black pepper, and toss gently over the heat.

5. Serve at once with the toasted pine nuts sprinkled over the top.

 QUICK COOK

Cod and Spinach with Gremolata

So easy and so tasty, this will become a go-to weekday supper dish. Panko breadcrumbs are easy to find and are crispier than regular breadcrumbs. Gremolata is a classic mix of grated lemon zest, garlic and parsley; we've added breadcrumbs to make it lovely and crisp. The flavours really enhance the dish.

Serves 4

Butter, for greasing

Gremolata
1 tbsp olive oil
30g (1oz) panko breadcrumbs
2 garlic cloves, finely grated
55g (2oz) Parmesan,
    finely grated
Finely grated zest of 1 lemon
1 tbsp freshly chopped
    parsley

225g (8oz) baby spinach
4 x 150g (5oz) cod
    loins, skinned
300ml (½ pint) pouring
    double cream
2 tbsp grainy mustard

Mary's Tips

The spinach and cod can be assembled up to 6 hours ahead. Add the sauce and gremolata just before cooking.

Not suitable for freezing.

1. Preheat the oven to 200°C/ Fan 180°C/Gas 6. Butter a round 30cm (12in) shallow ovenproof dish.

2. To make the gremolata, heat the oil in a frying pan over a high heat. Add the breadcrumbs and garlic and fry for a few minutes until lightly golden. Tip into a bowl. Add the Parmesan, lemon zest and parsley, and mix together.

3. Put the spinach leaves into a colander. Pour over a kettle of boiling water until the spinach has wilted. Refresh under cold water to stop the cooking and keep the bright green colour. Squeeze out as much liquid as you can.

4. Arrange the spinach in four piles on the base of the prepared dish. Place a piece of cod on each pile of spinach and season with salt and freshly ground black pepper.

5. Mix the cream, mustard and a little seasoning together in a small bowl. Divide the sauce between the cod loins, then spoon the gremolata on top. Bake in the preheated oven for about 18–20 minutes (depending on the thickness of the cod loins), until just cooked. The flesh should be white (not opaque) all the way through. If liquid comes out of the fish, it is cooked.

6. Serve hot with a green vegetable and baby new potatoes.

 ONE POT

Side of Salmon with Hoisin Vegetables

*A side of salmon is so impressive for a party. This recipe has a few parts
to it but is very easy and has wonderful East Asian flavours.*

Serves 10

Butter, for greasing

1.25kg (2lb 12oz) side
of salmon, skinned

5cm (2in) piece of fresh root
ginger, peeled and sliced

1 lemon, sliced

115g (4oz) mangetout

1 cucumber, peeled, cut
in half and deseeded

1 large carrot, peeled
and thinly sliced
into matchsticks

6 spring onions, trimmed
and thinly sliced
into matchsticks

10 radishes, thinly sliced

Bunch of coriander,
leaves finely chopped

Hoisin Dressing

3 tbsp sunflower oil

½ tsp toasted sesame oil

1 tbsp pickled ginger from
a jar, finely chopped

2 tbsp hoisin sauce

1 tbsp rice or white vinegar

2 tsp dark soy sauce

Juice of ½ lime

2 tsp caster sugar

Sweet Chilli Sauce

115g (4oz) mayonnaise

2 tbsp sweet chilli sauce

3 tbsp coriander leaves,
finely chopped

1. Preheat the oven to 180°C/Fan 160°C/Gas 4. Line a large roasting tin with a piece of buttered foil.

2. Place the salmon in the middle of the foil and season well with salt and freshly ground black pepper. Scatter the sliced fresh root ginger and lemon all around, then fold over the foil and seal to make a parcel. Place in the preheated oven and bake for about 25–30 minutes, until just cooked. The fish should be opaque. Remove from the oven and leave to become cold, keeping the foil parcel sealed.

3. Thinly slice the mangetout, then blanch in boiling salted water for 2 minutes. Drain and refresh in cold water. Cut the cucumber halves into crescent-shaped slices.

4. Place the mangetout and cucumber in a large bowl with the other vegetables and half the coriander.

5. Mix the hoisin dressing ingredients together in a jug. Pour the dressing over the vegetables and mix to combine.

6. To make the sweet chilli sauce, mix the ingredients together in a small bowl with the remaining coriander.

7. Carefully transfer the salmon onto a serving platter, discarding the ginger and lemon slices. Arrange a neat line of vegetables along the centre of the fish. Serve the remaining vegetables in a bowl alongside with the sweet chilli sauce.

Mary's Tips

Salmon can be cooked up to 6 hours ahead, serve on the same day. Dressing and sauce can be made up to 4 days ahead.

Tip the vegetables in the dressing just before serving. If you dress them too early, the vegetables will lose their crispness.

Not suitable for freezing.

 FOR A CROWD

Posh Salmon and Prawn Fishcakes with Tomato Salsa

One of my favourite supper dishes. I make these ahead, individually wrap each fishcake and freeze them. Then it's easy to remove two from the freezer, or however many you need, and defrost and cook for a no-fuss meal. Super easy.

Makes 8–10

250g (9oz) salmon fillet

2 knobs of butter

Large bunch of parsley

500g (1lb 2oz) potatoes, peeled and diced

175g (6oz) cooked tiger prawns, roughly chopped

4 tbsp mayonnaise

115g (4oz) panko breadcrumbs

2 tsp Dijon mustard

Juice of ½ small lemon

4 spring onions, trimmed and finely chopped

55g (2oz) Cheddar, grated

1 egg

Vegetable oil, for frying

75g (3oz) baby spinach (per person)

Tomato Salsa

6 tomatoes, seeds removed, finely chopped

1 small red onion, finely chopped

2 tsp sun-dried tomato paste

2 tbsp olive oil

1 tbsp fresh lemon juice

 FREEZES WELL

1. Preheat the oven to 200°C/180°C Fan/Gas 6.

2. Place the salmon fillet on a piece of foil and put a knob of butter on top. Break the parsley stalks from the bunch and sit them alongside the fillet. Fold over the foil to make a parcel. Bake the salmon in the preheated oven for about 15 minutes, or until cooked. Leave to cool, then remove and discard the skin. Flake the fish into small pieces. Save any buttery juices.

3. Meanwhile, cook the potatoes in boiling salted water until tender. Drain and mash, then leave to cool.

4. Spoon the mashed potato, salmon, any fish juices and the prawns into a large bowl. Add the mayo, 30g (1oz) of the breadcrumbs, the mustard, lemon juice, spring onions and cheese.

5. Chop the parsley leaves and set aside 1 tablespoon for the salsa. Add the remaining parsley to the bowl with the potato and fish. Season well with salt and freshly ground black pepper and mix together. Divide into 8–10 portions, then shape into fishcakes.

6. Crack the egg into a shallow dish and beat well. Scatter the remaining panko breadcrumbs onto a plate. Dip the fishcakes in the egg, then into the breadcrumbs to coat. If you are going to keep some or all of the fishcakes for another day, freeze them at this point.

7. To make the tomato salsa, add all the ingredients and the reserved parsley to a bowl. Season well and mix.

Mary's Tips

*Fishcakes and salsa can
be made a day ahead.*

Fishcakes freeze well uncooked.

8. Heat a little oil in a frying pan over a high heat. Add the fishcakes and fry for about 5–8 minutes on each side, until golden brown and crisp. Set aside.

9. Add the remaining knob of butter and the baby spinach to the pan, and cook over a high heat for 1 minute. Season well and stir until wilted.

10. Place the spinach on individual plates, sit a fishcake on top and serve a spoonful of the salsa alongside.

Goat's Cheese, Asparagus and Smoked Salmon Tarts

These look so attractive and are easy to make in large numbers.
Serve them warm – pastry is always best served warm!

Serves 6

18 fine asparagus spears

1 × 375g packet ready-rolled puff pastry

1 egg, beaten

2 × 150g (5oz) rolls, or tub, soft goat's cheese

50ml (2fl oz) pouring double cream

2 tsp freshly chopped thyme

1 tbsp freshly chopped chives

1 tsp Dijon mustard

200g (7oz) smoked salmon slices

Juice of ½ lemon

Mary's Tips

Can be made up to 4 hours ahead and warmed to serve. Decorate with smoked salmon just before serving.

Not suitable for freezing.

1. Preheat the oven to 200°C/Fan 180°C/Gas 6. Line a large flat baking sheet with non-stick baking paper.

2. Cook the asparagus in boiling salted water for 3 minutes. Drain and refresh in cold water. Drain again and dry thoroughly on kitchen paper. Cut the spears so they are about 8–9cm (3–3½in) long, then slice the remaining stems into small pieces.

3. Unroll the pastry sheet onto a floured work surface. Slice the pastry in half lengthways to make two long strips, each about 10cm (4in) wide. Place the strips onto the prepared baking sheet and prick the bases with a fork.

4. Brush the edges of the pastry with the beaten egg, then put the remaining egg into a large mixing bowl. Add the goat's cheese, double cream, herbs and mustard, and season with salt and freshly ground black pepper. Mix well, then stir in the small asparagus pieces. Spoon this mixture over the two pastry bases, leaving a 1.5cm (⅝in) border. Bake in the preheated oven for about 18–20 minutes, until lightly golden and set.

5. Remove the tarts from the oven and arrange the asparagus spears and smoked salmon slices over the tops of the tarts in a pretty design. Squeeze over the lemon juice and sprinkle with a little sea salt and black pepper to serve.

 QUICK COOK

Sea bream with Samphire and Chive Cream Sauce

A simple fish recipe that makes the most of delicious seabream. It is a quick recipe for a special supper. Sea bass and sea bream are often compared, but they are quite different. Sea bass is a delicate white fish, while sea bream has a more meaty, dense, flaky texture. Both are delicious and would work well here. Samphire is naturally salty, so go easy on the seasoning. Spinach or asparagus would work well if you can't get samphire.

Serves 4

4 sea bream fillets, skin on
2 tbsp sunflower oil
Knob of butter
300g (10½oz) samphire
½ lemon, cut into
   wedges, to serve

Chive Cream Sauce

200ml (⅓ pint) pouring
   double cream
2 tsp Dijon mustard
Juice of ½ lemon
2 tbsp freshly chopped chives

Mary's Tips

Best made and served. The sauce can be made up to 2 days ahead.

Not suitable for freezing.

1. To make the chive cream sauce, measure the cream and mustard into a small saucepan. Bring up to the boil, then add the lemon juice and chives, and season well with salt and freshly ground black pepper. Set aside.

2. Pat the sea bream fillets with kitchen paper to remove excess moisture, then season on both sides.

3. Heat the oil in a large frying pan over a medium-high heat. Add the butter and, when foaming, add the fillets, skin-side down. Push down firmly and fry for about 3 minutes, until the skin is crispy and the fish is nearly cooked. Turn the fillets, reduce the heat and cook for 1–2 minutes, until just cooked through.

4. Meanwhile, cook the samphire in boiling water for 3 minutes until just tender. Drain.

5. Warm the sauce through, and spoon some on to four warm plates. Place a fillet on top and the samphire on the side. Serve with lemon wedges and the remaining sauce alongside.

 QUICK COOK

All-in-one Lemon Pepper Cod

An all-in-one dish is perfect for making ahead. This can be made with sea bass fillets, too, but they can be thinner than cod so may need less time to cook. Choose equal-sized fillets so they cook at the same rate.

Serves 6

Butter, for greasing
6 × 150g (5oz) cod
    loins, skinned
1 lemon, thinly sliced

Pepper Sauce

2 tbsp olive oil
2 large onions, finely chopped
2 Romano peppers,
    deseeded and sliced
2 large garlic cloves,
    finely grated
1 × 400g tin chopped
    tomatoes
1 tbsp sun-dried tomato paste
2 tbsp capers from
    a jar, drained

Herb Sauce

115g (4oz) mayonnaise
1 garlic clove, finely grated
1 tbsp freshly chopped dill
1 tbsp freshly chopped
    parsley
1 tbsp capers from a jar,
    drained and chopped

Mary's Tips

*Can be assembled up
to 4 hours ahead.*

Not suitable for freezing.

1. Preheat the oven to 200°C/Fan 180°C/Gas 6 and butter a wide, shallow ovenproof dish.

2. To make the pepper sauce, heat the olive oil in a frying pan over a medium heat. Add the onions and peppers and fry for about 3–4 minutes. Add the garlic and fry for 10 seconds. Stir in the chopped tomatoes, tomato paste and capers, season with salt and freshly ground black pepper and cover with a lid. Simmer over a low heat for about 15 minutes, or until the onions are tender.

3. To make the herb sauce, mix all the ingredients together in a bowl.

4. Spoon the pepper sauce into the prepared ovenproof dish. Top with the cod fillets and season. Spoon the herb sauce on top of the fish, then scatter over the lemon slices. Bake in the preheated oven for about 20–25 minutes, or until the fish is just cooked through and the sauce is bubbling.

5. Serve hot with rice, green vegetables and herb sauce.

 ONE POT

Tiger Prawn and Coriander Courgetti

A super healthy and quick supper. By using a spiralizer, the courgette becomes like spaghetti but with fewer carbs! If you only have large courgettes, cut them in half lengthways and scoop out the seeds before spiralizing. It is essential to try and serve immediately, otherwise the courgettes lose their texture and become watery.

Serves 2

6 small courgettes

3 tbsp olive oil

6 spring onions, trimmed and sliced

½ red chilli, deseeded and finely chopped

3 large garlic cloves, finely grated

150g (5oz) cooked tiger prawns

Juice of ½ small lemon

2 tbsp freshly chopped coriander

Mary's Tips

Make and serve.

Not suitable for freezing.

1. Slice the courgettes in half lengthways then put them through a spiralizer to make long courgette spaghetti.

2. Place a large frying pan over a high heat until very hot. Add the oil, spring onions, chilli and garlic and fry for 10 seconds. Add the prawns and season with salt and freshly ground black pepper. Fry for 1–2 minutes to heat through.

3. Add two thirds of the courgetti and the lemon juice with more seasoning, and fry quickly over the high heat for 1 minute, or until just wilted.

4. Turn off the heat, add the remaining courgetti (this will add to the texture) and the coriander and toss together.

5. Serve at once in warm bowls.

 QUICK COOK

Crispy Squid with Aioli

Often when you enjoy squid rings at a taverna in the Mediterranean, they'll have batter around them and are deep fried. I do not deep fry, so I am always trying out different ways to make favourite recipes without that process. This works rather well!

Serves 4–6

75g (3oz) plain flour
¼ tsp paprika
175g (9oz) semolina
2 eggs
300g (10½oz) squid rings
2 tbsp sunflower oil
75g (3oz) butter

Aioli

115g (4oz) mayonnaise
Juice of ½ lemon
1 garlic clove, finely grated
1 tsp Dijon mustard

Mary's Tips

Best made and served. Aioli can be made up to 2 days ahead but the flavour will become stronger with age!

Not suitable for freezing.

1. To make the aioli, mix the ingredients in a bowl and season well with salt and freshly ground black pepper.

2. Measure the flour and paprika onto a plate and mix together. Tip the semolina onto a separate plate. Break the eggs into a bowl and beat with a fork.

3. Pat the squid rings dry with kitchen paper and season well. Toss the squid in the flour, then dip in the beaten egg and finally roll in semolina. Do this in batches until all the squid rings are well coated. Line a plate with kitchen paper.

4. Heat 1 tablespoon of oil and half the butter in a large frying pan over a high heat. Put half the squid into the frying pan, well-spaced apart. Fry for about 1–2 minutes until golden, then turn and fry on the other side until golden and crisp. Place on the plate lined with kitchen paper.

5. Wipe the frying pan with kitchen paper before repeating the process with the remaining oil, butter and squid.

6. Pile the crispy squid into a bowl and serve, ideally straight away, with the aioli alongside.

 QUICK COOK

Chicken

Easy Peasy One-pot Chicken

A whole spatchcock chicken with Mediterranean-style vegetables, this is a healthy and hearty all-in-one dish made in a casserole or deep saucepan. Removing the backbone of the chicken makes it a spatchcock and it is easier to arrange in the pot and to carve or joint. Double up for eight people, if you wish, and arrange two chickens in a large roasting tin, covered in foil.

Serves 4–6

2 tbsp olive oil

1 large onion, thinly sliced

1 large fennel bulb, thinly sliced

1 red pepper, deseeded and diced

3 large garlic cloves, finely grated

100ml (3½fl oz) white wine

1 x 400g tin chopped tomatoes

2 tbsp sun-dried tomato paste

2 tsp Worcestershire sauce

1 small whole chicken (about 1.25kg/2lb 12oz)

5 bay leaves

1 lemon, thinly sliced into rounds

1 tsp paprika

1 tbsp runny honey

Mary's Tips

Prepare the vegetables ahead. Bring the veg back to the boil before adding the chicken and cooking in the oven.

Not suitable for freezing.

1. Preheat the oven to 200°C/180°C Fan/Gas 6.

2. Heat the oil in a deep lidded casserole or large, lidded, ovenproof frying pan over a high heat. Add the onion, fennel and pepper and fry for about 3–4 minutes, stirring regularly. Add the garlic and fry for 30 seconds. Pour in the wine and boil to reduce by half.

3. Stir in the chopped tomatoes, sun-dried tomato paste and Worcestershire sauce, and season with salt and black pepper.

4. Meanwhile, put the chicken upside down on a board. Remove the backbone by cutting either side of the bone with scissors. Turn over and press down on the breastbone to flatten the bird; it is now a spatchcock chicken. Arrange the lemon slices and bay leaves over the chicken.

5. Put the chicken, breast-side up, on top of the vegetables in the casserole or frying pan. Season and bring up to the boil. Cover with a lid and transfer to the preheated oven for about 35 minutes.

6. Remove the lid and sprinkle the paprika over the chicken and drizzle with the honey. Return to the oven, uncovered, for about 30 minutes to brown and finish cooking.

7. To serve, spoon the vegetables on to a hot platter and joint or carve the chicken before arranging the chicken on top of the vegetables.

 ONE POT

Hoisin Chicken with Pancakes

Think of crispy duck in a smart Chinese restaurant – this is a take on that. Using a whole roast chicken with Chinese flavours, this recipe is not crispy but tender and fun to make. Lucinda, who helps us, did this for her son Henry's 10th birthday party and all the children loved it! Rice pancakes can be bought easily in supermarkets or delis.

Serves 6–8

1 x 1.5kg (3lb 5oz) whole chicken

20–30 small Chinese rice pancakes

½ large cucumber, deseeded and thinly sliced into matchsticks

Large bunch of spring onions, trimmed and thinly sliced into matchsticks

2 large carrots, peeled and thinly sliced into matchsticks

Marinade

2 tbsp hoisin sauce, plus extra to serve

2 tsp tomato purée

2 tbsp Chinese five spice powder

3 tbsp soy sauce

2 tbsp runny honey

2 tsp rice or white wine vinegar

1 large garlic clove, finely grated

Mary's Tips

Chicken can be marinated a day ahead.

Chicken freezes well raw and marinated.

1. Measure all the marinade ingredients into a large dish. Mix well, then add the chicken. Using your hands, rub the marinade into the chicken and leave to marinate in the fridge for 1–4 hours.

2. Preheat the oven to 200°C/180°C Fan/Gas 6 and line a roasting tin with non-stick baking paper.

3. Place the chicken in the prepared tin and season well with salt and freshly ground black pepper. Pour any excess marinade from the bowl over the chicken. Roast in the oven for about 1–1¼ hours, covering the chicken with foil after the first 30 minutes, until cooked through. Expect it to be very dark brown, almost black, but not burnt. Leave the chicken to rest for 15 minutes, covered in the foil.

4. Warm the pancakes in a steamer or a microwave according to the packet instructions.

5. Carve the chicken into slices and shred the leg meat. Arrange the chicken, pancakes and prepared vegetables in the centre of the table with a small bowl of hoisin sauce on the side. Everyone can help themselves!

6. To serve, spread a little hoisin sauce on a pancake, then place some chicken and vegetables in the centre. Roll up tightly to make a small roll.

 PREP AHEAD

Chicken Tartiflette

A take on the classic tartiflette, which is a dish of potato, bacon, onions and Reblochon cheese traditional in the Alps. Choose a smoked cured ham of your choice. If you can't find Reblochon, use Brie or Camembert instead.

Serves 6

8 slices Parma or Black Forest ham

2 onions, thinly sliced

500g (1lb 2oz) new potatoes, thickly sliced

2 tbsp olive oil

2 garlic cloves, finely grated

6 small skinless boneless chicken breasts

200g (7oz) button mushrooms

200ml (⅓ pint) white wine

150ml (¼ pint) pouring double cream

115g (4oz) Reblochon cheese, rind removed and diced

1 tbsp grainy mustard

Juice of ½ lemon

1 tbsp freshly chopped thyme

2 tbsp freshly chopped parsley

Mary's Tips

The first stage of cooking the vegetables, before adding the chicken, can be made up to 2 hours ahead.

Not suitable for freezing.

1. Preheat the oven to 200°C/180°C Fan/Gas 6.

2. Snip two slices of the Parma ham into small pieces.

3. Put the snipped Parma ham, onions, potatoes, oil and garlic into a large, shallow roasting tin. Season with salt and freshly ground black pepper and toss everything together. Roast in the preheated oven for about 25 minutes, until the potato slices are nearly tender.

4. Meanwhile, put the remaining slices of Parma ham on a board. Place the chicken breasts on top of the ham and wrap one around each breast. Season.

5. Remove the roasting tin from the oven. Stir in the mushrooms, wine and cream, and add the cheese. Sit the wrapped chicken breasts on top of the vegetables and return to the oven for about 20–22 minutes, or until the chicken and vegetables are tender.

6. Remove the chicken from the tin and place on a warm plate to rest. Stir the mustard, lemon juice and herbs into the tin until combined.

7. Carve each chicken breast into three, spoon over the vegetables and sauce, and serve piping hot with a green vegetable alongside.

 ONE POT

Chicken and Ham Burgundy Pie

The ultimate chicken pie, with leeks and mushrooms and a rich sauce. Serve with fresh vegetables. If you haven't any Burgundy, use a robust red wine.

Serves 6

55g (2oz) butter

2 banana shallots, thinly sliced

3 leeks, thinly sliced

200g (7oz) small chestnut mushrooms, sliced

1 garlic clove, finely grated

55g (2oz) plain flour

250ml (9fl oz) Burgundy red wine

350ml (12fl oz) chicken stock

1–2 tbsp Worcestershire sauce

1 tbsp redcurrant jelly

2 tbsp freshly chopped thyme

A little gravy browning

350g (12oz) cooked ham, diced

350g (12oz) cooked chicken, diced

1 × 320g packet ready-rolled puff pastry

1 egg, beaten

Mary's Tips

The pie can be prepared completely up to 8 hours ahead. Bring to room temperature to cook.

Freezes well uncooked.

1. Melt the butter in a large, deep frying pan over a high heat. Add the shallots and leeks and fry for about 5–8 minutes, until nearly soft. Add the mushrooms and garlic and fry for 1 minute.

2. Measure the flour into a bowl or large jug. Slowly pour in the red wine, whisking all the time, until smooth. Add the stock and mix well. Pour the wine and stock mixture into the pan with the mushrooms and stir over the heat until thickened.

3. Add the Worcestershire sauce, redcurrant jelly, thyme and browning, season with salt and freshly ground pepper and simmer for 5 minutes. Remove from the heat and set aside to cool.

4. Add the chicken and ham, stir and check the seasoning. Spoon into an overproof dish and chill in the fridge.

5. Preheat the oven to 200°C/180°C Fan/Gas 6.

6. Unroll the pastry. Wet the inside of the dish above the filling with water. Lay the pastry over the filling and press a lip into the sides of the dish. Trim the top and score the surface to make a neat pattern. Make a small slit in the centre for the steam to escape. Brush the surface with the beaten egg and bake in the preheated oven for about 35–40 minutes, until the filling is hot and the pastry is cooked and golden brown.

 PREP AHEAD

Chicken Escalope with Tzatziki

A quick supper dish, great for sharing. Tzatziki is a Greek and middle European dip – I love it and spread it on toast and top it with avocado! These escalopes would go well with the Quinoa and Soya Bean Salad with Preserved Lemon Dressing on page 177.

Serves 4

2 large skinless boneless
  chicken breasts
2 tsp dried mustard powder
1 tbsp freshly chopped
  parsley
1 tbsp freshly chopped dill
1–2 tbsp sunflower oil

Tzatziki

200g (7oz) Greek yoghurt
1 garlic clove, finely grated
½ cucumber, deseeded
  and coarsely grated
3 tbsp freshly chopped mint

Mary's Tips

*Tzatziki can be made
up to 3 days ahead.*

Not suitable for freezing.

1. Put the chicken breasts onto a board. Slice each breast in two horizontally through the middle. Lay a piece of baking paper over the chicken breasts and bash with a rolling pin until you have a thin escalope.

2. Remove the baking paper and sprinkle both sides of the breasts with the mustard powder, parsley and dill and season with salt and freshly ground black pepper. Drizzle the oil over the top.

3. Heat a frying pan until very hot. Add the chicken breasts and fry for 2 minutes on each side until golden brown and just cooked through. Set aside to rest for a few minutes.

4. Meanwhile, to make the tzatziki, mix the yoghurt, garlic, cucumber and mint together in a bowl. Season with salt and freshly ground black pepper.

5. Serve the golden chicken with the dip alongside.

QUICK COOK

Chicken Satay-style Curry

Satay chicken is a classic Indonesian dish and is often served as skewers of chicken with the peanut dipping sauce on the side. Here we have incorporated the flavours into a curry. If you are unable to buy mini fillets, buy two fillets and cut each into three long pieces.

Serves 4

2 tsp ground coriander
2 tsp ground cumin
1 tbsp mild curry powder
675g (1½lb) mini chicken fillets
2½ tbsp sweet chilli sauce
4 tbsp sunflower oil
1 large onion, finely chopped
2 garlic cloves, finely grated
1 tbsp finely grated fresh root ginger
75g (3oz) smooth peanut butter
1 × 400ml can full-fat coconut milk
75ml (2½fl oz) water
1 tbsp soy sauce
Juice of 1 lime
A few coriander leaves, to garnish

Mary's Tips

Can be made completely up to a day ahead. You may need to add a little more water to thin the sauce when you reheat.

Freezes well.

1. Measure the ground coriander, ground cumin and curry powder into a medium bowl. Mix together, then spoon half of the spices into a separate small bowl and set aside.

2. Add the chicken to the medium bowl with 1 teaspoon of the sweet chilli sauce. Season well with salt and freshly ground black pepper and toss to coat.

3. Heat 2 tablespoons of the oil in a large frying pan, or a deep lidded casserole, over a high heat. Add the chicken and brown until golden all over, but still raw inside (you may need to do this in batches). Remove from the pan and set aside.

4. Wipe the pan of any burnt residue, then add the remaining oil and the onion and fry over a high heat for 5 minutes. Stir in the garlic, ginger and the spices in the small bowl, and fry for 10 seconds. Add all the remaining ingredients, including the remaining sweet chilli sauce, stir until smooth, and bring up to the boil.

5. Return the chicken to the pan, cover with a lid, reduce the heat and simmer for about 8 minutes, or until the chicken is cooked through. Add a little more water if the sauce is too thick.

6. Garnish with some coriander leaves and serve piping hot with rice.

 ONE POT

Creamy Lemon Tarragon Chicken

This is a cold main dish, perfect to feed a crowd. It's really worth poaching the chicken to add flavour and give the best tender chicken. Choose a pan which will fit the chicken comfortably and the water will just cover.

Serves 6

2 lemons, cut into wedges
4 bay leaves
6 black peppercorns
1 large chicken

Lemon and Tarragon Sauce

4 preserved lemons, roughly chopped and pips removed
4 tbsp mayonnaise
500g (1lb 2oz) half-fat crème fraîche
Juice of ½ lemon
2 tbsp freshly chopped tarragon, plus extra to garnish
4 tbsp freshly chopped parsley
4 celery sticks, trimmed and finely chopped

Mary's Tips

Can be made up to a day ahead.

Not suitable for freezing.

1. To poach the chicken, put the fresh lemon wedges, bay leaves, peppercorns and chicken into a large saucepan. Cover with cold water and a lid and bring up to the boil. Cook for 3–4 minutes, then lower the heat and simmer gently for about 50 minutes, until the chicken is cooked through. Remove the lid and leave to cool in the water. Drain, reserving the liquid to use as stock another day. Leave the chicken to cool completely.

2. To make the lemon and tarragon sauce, put the preserved lemons in a food processor and whiz until finely chopped. Add the mayonnaise, crème fraîche, lemon juice and herbs and whiz until smooth. Transfer to a large bowl, season with salt and freshly ground black pepper and stir in the chopped celery.

3. Remove the skin from the chicken and slice the meat into pieces. Discard the bones. Add the cold chicken to the sauce and mix well. Cover and chill in the fridge for 2 hours or overnight.

4. Sprinkle with some more fresh tarragon and serve as a cold dish with new potatoes or rice.

 PREP AHEAD

Harissa Chicken and Red Rice Salad

Aromatic, fragrant and bursting with flavour. Red rice has a wonderful colour and is full of nutrients. It also has fewer carbohydrates than other types of rice.

Serves 6

3 skinless boneless chicken
  breasts, sliced into strips
4 tbsp olive oil
2 tbsp white wine vinegar
Finely grated zest and
  juice of 3 lemons
1 tsp harissa paste
2 tbsp sun-dried tomato paste
6 carrots, peeled and
  coarsely grated
2 celery sticks, trimmed
  and diced
6 spring onions,
  trimmed and sliced
450g (1lb) red rice
Small bunch of coriander,
  leaves roughly chopped

Marinade

1 tbsp ground cumin
2 tbsp sun-dried tomato paste
½ tsp harissa paste
1 tbsp sunflower oil

Mary's Tips

*Can be made and assembled
up to 4 hours ahead.*

Not suitable for freezing.

1. To make the marinade, measure all the ingredients into a bowl and stir to combine. Add the chicken strips, season well with salt and freshly ground black pepper and mix until the chicken is coated. Leave to marinate for at least 30 minutes.

2. Measure the olive oil, vinegar, lemon zest and juice, harissa and tomato paste into a large bowl. Mix together, then stir in the carrot, celery and spring onions.

3. Cook the rice according to the packet instructions, then drain well and add to the vegetables in the bowl. Stir well and check the seasoning.

4. Heat a large frying pan over a high heat. Add the chicken and fry for about 4 minutes until brown and cooked through.

5. Stir the coriander into the rice, then spoon into a serving dish. Arrange the chicken on top to serve.

 PREP AHEAD

Italian Chicken

An all-in-one dish ready to slide into the oven. All the flavours of Italy in one dish. If preferred, use Gorgonzola instead of Dolcelatte.

Serves 4

150g (5oz) Dolcelatte
  cheese, cubed
4 tbsp sun-dried tomato paste
2 garlic cloves, finely grated
4 tbsp freshly chopped basil
30g (1oz) panko breadcrumbs
300g (10½oz) passata
4 small skinless boneless
  chicken breasts

Mary's Tips

*Can be assembled up
to 6 hours ahead.*

Not suitable for freezing.

1. Preheat the oven to 200°C/180°C Fan/Gas 6. You will need a small ovenproof dish or roasting tin.

2. To make the filling, put the cheese in a bowl and mash with a fork. Add 2 tablespoons of the sun-dried tomato paste, half the grated garlic, half the basil and half the panko breadcrumbs. Mash together and season well with salt and freshly ground black pepper.

3. Measure the passata into a jug and add the remaining tomato paste, garlic and basil. Season well, then pour the sauce into the base of a shallow, ovenproof dish.

4. Make a slit in the middle of each chicken breast about a quarter of the way through to open a pocket in the breast. Press the cheese mixture into the opening and on top of the breast, then sprinkle with the remaining breadcrumbs.

5. Sit the chicken breasts on top of the sauce in the dish and season well. Bake in the preheated oven for about 30–35 minutes, until golden on top and the chicken is cooked through.

 ONE POT

Lucinda's Chicken Curry

Our lovely Lucinda, who has worked with us for over 20 years, used to be full time and now comes in and tests recipes once a week, as she is a mother of two. She is a treasure, and has a wealth of experience gathered over the years. This curry is packed with spices and aromatic flavours, and is one she has perfected.

Serves 6

4 tbsp sunflower oil

1.25kg (2lb 12oz) skinless chicken thigh fillets, diced

3 large onions, thinly sliced

2 large garlic cloves, finely grated

Large piece of fresh root ginger, peeled and finely grated

30g (1oz) plain flour

1 tbsp garam masala

1 tbsp ground cumin

1 tbsp medium curry powder

¼ tsp ground allspice

2 tsp ground turmeric

450ml (¾ pint) chicken stock

150ml (¼ pint) pouring double cream

1–2 tbsp mango chutney

Mary's Tips

Can be made up to a day ahead and reheated to serve.

Freezes well cooked.

1. Heat 2 tablespoons of the oil in a large, deep frying pan over a high heat. Season the chicken with salt and freshly ground black pepper, then add to the pan and fry until browned. Set aside.

2. Heat the remaining oil in the pan, add the onions and fry for 5 minutes. Add the garlic and ginger and fry for a few seconds. Sprinkle in the flour and all the spices and fry for 10 seconds.

3. Mix in the stock, stirring all the time, and bring up to the boil to make a thick sauce.

4. Return the chicken, and any juices on the plate, to the pan, cover with a lid and bring back to the boil. Reduce the heat and simmer for 45 minutes over a low heat, stirring from time to time, until tender.

5. Stir in the double cream and mango chutney, and check the seasoning. Serve with rice and poppadoms.

 PREP AHEAD

Chicken Legs with
Smoky Bulgur Wheat

Best to start this the day before, to give time for all the flavours to infuse.

Serves 6

6 chicken legs

Marinade
3 tbsp olive oil
Zest and juice of 1 lemon
2 garlic cloves, finely grated
2 tsp smoked paprika

Smoky Bulgur Wheat
2 tbsp olive oil
1 onion, finely chopped
½ red pepper, deseeded
  and diced
55g (2oz) chorizo slices,
  roughly chopped
2 garlic cloves, finely grated
1 tsp smoked paprika
1 tbsp tomato purée
300g (10½oz) bulgur wheat
500ml (18fl oz) chicken stock
5 sun-dried tomatoes,
  finely chopped
Small bunch of dill, chopped
Small bunch of parsley,
  leaves chopped
Juice of ½ lemon

Mary's Tips

*Can be made up to a day
ahead and served cold.*

Not suitable for freezing.

1. The day before, measure all the marinade ingredients into a bowl and mix well. Put the chicken legs into the marinade and rub it into the chicken. Leave in the fridge overnight, or for at least an hour.

2. Preheat the oven to 220°C/Fan 200°C/Gas 7.

3. Put the chicken legs in a roasting tin and season well with salt and freshly ground black pepper. Roast in the preheated oven for about 35–45 minutes, or until cooked through, basting from time to time. Remove from the oven, cover with foil and set aside to rest.

4. To make the smoky bulgur wheat, heat the oil in a shallow wide-based pan over a high heat. Add the onion, pepper and chorizo and fry for 5 minutes until starting to turn golden. Add the garlic, paprika, purée and bulgur wheat and stir. Pour in the stock, add the sun-dried tomatoes and season with salt and freshly ground black pepper. Cover with a lid and bring up to the boil. Boil for 3 minutes, then turn off the heat and leave to stand for about 15 minutes, until all of the liquid has been absorbed and the bulgur wheat is cooked. Stir in the dill, parsley and lemon juice and check the seasoning.

5. Transfer the bulgur wheat to a platter, place the chicken legs on top and drizzle some of the roasting juices over the chicken legs to serve with a small green salad.

 PREP AHEAD

Chicken and Broccoli Stir-fry

Bursting with flavour and fresh ingredients, this will become a firm favourite with the family. Serve on its own or with noodles or rice.

Serves 4

2 skinless boneless
   chicken breasts, cut
   into long, thin strips
1 tbsp runny honey
2 tbsp olive oil
250g (9oz) tenderstem
   broccoli, halved if large
175g (6oz) baby corn,
   halved lengthways
1 carrot, peeled and
   cut into strips
1 spring onion, trimmed
   and finely chopped
150g (5oz) chestnut
   mushrooms, quartered
1 small red chilli, deseeded
   and finely chopped
2 garlic cloves, finely grated
75ml (3fl oz) white wine
Juice of ½ lemon
3 tbsp freshly chopped basil

Mary's Tips

Best made and served.

Not suitable for freezing.

1. Place the chicken in a bowl and drizzle with the honey. Season with salt and freshly ground black pepper and turn to coat.

2. Heat 1 tablespoon of the oil in a frying pan over a high heat, add the chicken and fry for 2 minutes, turning until golden. Remove with a slotted spoon.

3. Add the remaining oil to the pan, then stir in the broccoli, baby corn and carrots and fry over a high heat for about 1–2 minutes. Add the spring onion, mushrooms, chilli and garlic, and fry for a further 2 minutes.

4. Return the chicken to the pan, pour in the wine and lemon juice and boil for 1 minute, stirring.

5. Remove from the heat, stir in the basil and serve in a large serving bowl.

 QUICK COOK

Pork, Beef and Lamb

Meatball Toad in the Hole with Sage

*Think of a classic toad in the hole, then replace the sausages with
herbed meatballs. You could also make it in a small roasting tin,
but it makes a nice change to cook it in a round pan.*

Serves 6

350g (12oz) pork
  sausage meat
30g (1oz) Parmesan, grated
1 tbsp freshly chopped sage
1 tsp Dijon mustard
4 spring onions, trimmed
  and finely chopped
4 tbsp plain flour
6 tbsp sunflower oil

Batter
115g (4oz) plain flour
4 large eggs
150ml (¼ pint) milk

Mary's Tips

*Brown the meatballs and mix
the batter up to 6 hours ahead.*

Meatballs freeze well uncooked.

1. Preheat the oven to 240°C/220°C Fan/Gas 9.

2. Put the sausage meat, Parmesan, sage, mustard and spring onions into a bowl. Season well with salt and freshly ground black pepper and, using your hands, knead together to mix the flavours. Shape into 20 equal-sized meatballs, then roll in the plain flour.

3. To make the batter, measure the flour into a bowl and make a little well in the centre. Break the eggs into the well and add a little of the milk. Whisk by hand, slowly adding the rest of the milk, until you have a smooth batter.

4. Heat 1 tablespoon of the oil in an ovenproof non-stick frying pan. Add the meatballs and brown over a high heat. Remove the meatballs from the pan and set aside.

5. Add the remaining oil to the pan and put the pan in the oven for 10 minutes to get hot.

6. When the oil is very hot, pour in the batter and place the meatballs on top. Bake in the preheated oven for about 25–30 minutes, until well risen and the batter is golden brown and crisp.

 ONE POT

Pork Tacos with Avocado Salsa

A great family supper. We use the shop-bought crisp taco shells, but you could use soft tacos, if preferred. The filling would work well in both.

Serves 6

2 tbsp sunflower oil

500g (1lb 2oz) lean minced pork

4 spring onions, trimmed and thinly sliced

1 green pepper, deseeded and finely diced

2 garlic cloves, finely grated

½ red chilli, deseeded and finely diced

1 tbsp each of paprika, ground cumin and ground coriander

1 tbsp mango chutney

Juice of ½ lime

12 crispy taco shells

Soured cream, to serve

Avocado Salsa

2 spring onions, trimmed and finely sliced

½ red chilli, deseeded and finely diced

2 firm ripe avocados, peeled and diced

Juice of 1 lime

Small bunch of coriander, leaves roughly chopped

2 tbsp olive oil

Mary's Tips

Pork mixture can be made up to 4 hours ahead. Salsa can be made 2 hours ahead.

Not suitable for freezing.

1. Heat the sunflower oil in a large frying pan over a high heat. Add the mince and fry until browned, breaking up with two wooden spoons as it fries.

2. Add the spring onions and pepper and fry for 3–4 minutes. Stir in the garlic, chilli and spices, and fry for 2–3 minutes until fragrant. Season with salt and freshly ground black pepper.

3. Stir in the mango chutney and lime juice, mix well and cover with a lid. Simmer over a low heat for about 5–7 minutes, until the pork is cooked through.

4. Meanwhile, mix the salsa ingredients together in a bowl, reserving some of the coriander to garnish, and season well.

5. Spoon the pork into the taco shells, top with some salsa, a dollop of soured cream and a sprinkle of coriander. Serve with a dressed salad alongside.

 QUICK COOK

Bacon and Mushroom Cheese Soufflé

Made all in one dish, this is perfect as a lunch or light supper. Best made and served at once.

Serves 4

30g (1oz) butter, plus extra for greasing

30g (1oz) plain flour

300ml (½ pint) hot milk

2 tsp Dijon mustard

55g (2oz) mature Cheddar, grated

55g (2oz) Parmesan, grated

3 large eggs, separated

2 tbsp freshly chopped parsley

200g (7oz) smoked bacon, sliced into small pieces

250g (9oz) chestnut mushrooms, thickly sliced

Mary's Tips

Not for freezing.

1. Preheat the oven to 220°C/200°C Fan/Gas 7. Grease a 23cm (9in) round ovenproof dish with butter. It will need to be about 5cm (2in) deep.

2. Melt the butter in a saucepan over a medium heat. Add the flour and stir for 30 seconds. Slowly pour in the milk, whisking all the time until thick and bubbling. Remove from the heat and add the mustard and both cheeses. Season well with salt and freshly ground black pepper. Cool slightly before stirring in the egg yolks and parsley.

3. Place a frying pan over a high heat. Add the bacon and fry for a few minutes. Add the mushrooms and fry until all the liquid has evaporated and the bacon is starting to crisp.

4. Meanwhile, whisk the egg whites in a large clean bowl with an electric hand whisk until stiff and cloud-like. Add a good tablespoon of beaten egg white and beat well into the cheese mixture, then gently fold the remaining egg white into the cheese mixture.

5. Transfer the hot bacon and mushrooms into the base of the prepared dish. Spoon the soufflé over the top. Bake in the preheated oven for about 15–18 minutes, until well risen, golden and just set in the middle.

6. Serve at once, with dressed salad leaves.

 QUICK COOK

Pork Chops with Mushroom Sauce

A simple weekday supper, quick to make with a delicious creamy sauce.

Serves 2

1 tbsp sunflower oil

2 thick-cut pork chops, rind removed

Knob of butter

150g (5oz) button mushrooms, sliced

100ml (3½fl oz) white wine

200ml (⅓ pint) pouring double cream

Squeeze of fresh lemon juice

3 tbsp freshly chopped chives

Mary's Tips

Not suitable for freezing.

1. Preheat the oven to 200°C/180°C Fan/Gas 6.

2. Place an ovenproof frying pan over a high heat until hot. Add the oil and fry the chops for 1–2 minutes on each side until brown. Transfer the pan to the preheated oven for about 5–10 minutes, or until the pork is cooked through (this will depend on the thickness of the chops).

3. Transfer the chops to a hot plate, cover with foil and leave to rest. Drain any juices into a bowl and reserve.

4. Return the pan to a medium heat. Add the butter and the mushrooms and fry for about 2–3 minutes, turning occasionally.

5. Pour in the wine and reduce by half over a high heat. Pour in the cream and reduce by half again until a coating consistency. Add the pork juices, lemon juice and chopped chives, and season with salt and freshly ground black pepper.

6. Place the chops on a serving plate and serve the mushroom sauce alongside.

 ONE POT

Miso Steak with Asparagus Salad

Buy your favourite cut of steak and use this delicious sweet and sour miso sauce as a marinade. Serve it with rocket salad and noodles or skinny fries. It is important to wipe the pan clean before cooking the vegetables, as the marinade residue in the pan may burn.

Serves 4

4 small steaks (rump or your favourite cut)

3 tbsp sunflower oil

½ tsp cornflour

Marinade

2 tbsp soy sauce

2 tbsp sweet chilli sauce

2 tsp white miso paste

2 tsp honey

2 tsp white wine vinegar

Vegetable Salad

2 carrots, peeled and thinly sliced into matchsticks

6 large spring onions, trimmed and thinly sliced into matchsticks

Small piece of fresh root ginger, peeled and sliced into matchsticks

8 extra-fine asparagus spears

2 tbsp toasted sesame seeds, to serve

Mary's Tips

Steak can be marinated up to a day ahead.

Raw steak freezes well marinated.

1. Measure all the marinade ingredients into a shallow dish. Mix well and add the steaks. Coat in the marinade and leave for 30 minutes to an hour to marinate.

2. Preheat a large frying pan over a medium-high heat.

3. Scrape excess marinade off the steaks and reserve in the dish. Season the steaks with salt and freshly ground black pepper and use 1–2 tablespoons of the oil to brush on the steaks. Fry in the hot pan for 2 minutes on each side to give a pink centre. Place on a warm plate to rest.

4. Wipe the pan clean and add the remaining oil. Add the vegetables and fry very quickly over a high heat for about 1 minute, until just wilted but with crunch.

5. Add 6 tablespoons of water and the cornflour to the reserved marinade in the dish. Mix well, then transfer to a small saucepan. Put the pan over a high heat and bring up to the boil, stirring until just thickened. Make sure you do not reduce the sauce by too much, as there is very little.

6. Serve the steak whole or carved into three diagonal slices with the vegetables alongside. Pour the sauce over the top and sprinkle with the sesame seeds.

 ONE POT

Beef and Aubergine Crunchy Top Filo Pie

A great dish for a gang – make it ahead and bake it to serve. You can replace the aubergine with courgettes, if preferred. Using filo pastry makes it a very easy topping. Freeze any leftover filo; just wrap it up well and it'll be ready for another occasion.

Serves 6–8

4 tbsp sunflower oil

2 onions, diced

400g (14oz) lean minced beef

3 garlic cloves, finely grated

1 tbsp tomato purée

2 × 400g tins chopped
tomatoes

½ tsp sugar

2 small aubergines, cut into
slices 1cm (½in) thick

1 × 280g tub full-fat
cream cheese

4 tbsp freshly chopped
parsley

1 tbsp freshly chopped thyme

Filo Topping

4 large sheets of filo pastry

30g (1oz) butter, melted

 PREP AHEAD

1. Preheat the oven to 200°C/180°C Fan/Gas 6 and line a large baking sheet with non-stick baking paper. You will also need a shallow round dish about 28cm (11in) wide (with a capacity of about 1.75 litres/3 pints).

2. Heat half the oil in a large frying pan over a medium heat. Add the onions and fry for 3–4 minutes. Add the mince and brown over a high heat, breaking up with two wooden spoons as it fries. Add two thirds of the garlic and fry for 30 seconds. Stir in the purée, chopped tomatoes and sugar, mix well and cover with a lid. Bring up to the boil, then reduce the heat and simmer for about 1 hour until tender.

3. Meanwhile, arrange the aubergine slices on the prepared baking sheet and drizzle with the remaining oil. Season with salt and freshly ground black pepper and roast in the preheated oven for about 20–25 minutes, turning halfway through, until lightly brown and soft.

4. Spoon the cream cheese into a bowl and mix with the remaining garlic and half the parsley. Season well.

5. Season the mince and stir in the thyme and the remaining parsley. Spoon half into the base of the round dish, then arrange a single layer of aubergine slices on top. Dot the cream cheese mixture over the aubergine and spread out a little. Top with the remaining mince.

6. Place the filo pastry on a work surface. Brush each sheet with melted butter, then cut the sheets in half, so you have eight pieces of filo.

7. Roughly scrunch the sheets and arrange them on top of the pie to cover the surface completely. Bake in the preheated oven for about 25–30 minutes, until the pastry is crisp and brown and the mince is bubbling.

Thai Basil Beef Stir-fry

Quick, easy and all in one dish. Mint would work well, if you can't find Thai basil.

Serves 6

Thai-style Sauce
2 tsp finely grated
   fresh root ginger
1 tbsp red Thai curry paste
1 x 160ml can of
   coconut cream
1 tbsp sweet chilli sauce
2 tbsp soy sauce
1 tsp light muscovado sugar
2 tsp cornflour

350g (12oz) rump steak,
sliced into long strips

Marinade
1 red chilli, deseeded
   and finely chopped
Juice of ½ lime
1 tbsp soy sauce

2 tbsp sunflower oil
175g (6oz) baby corn, cut
   into 3 lengthways
1 small yellow pepper,
   deseeded and thinly sliced
2 pak choi, sliced into chunks
1 onion, thinly sliced
2 tbsp freshly chopped
   Thai basil leaves

Mary's Tips

*Best made and served.
Beef can be marinated
up to 2 hours ahead.*

Not suitable for freezing.

1. Measure all the ingredients for the Thai-style sauce into a bowl and mix well.

2. Place the steak strips in a bowl. Add the marinade of chilli, lime juice and soy sauce. Mix to coat and leave to marinate for about 30 minutes.

3. Heat 1 tablespoon of the oil in a non-stick frying pan over a high heat. Remove the beef from its marinade using a slotted spoon and add to the pan. Fry for a few minutes until golden brown. Remove from the pan and set aside.

4. Add the remaining oil to the pan and the baby corn, pepper, pak choi and onion and fry over a high heat for about 3 minutes. Pour in the Thai-style sauce and reserved marinade, stirring for 2 minutes until thickened.

5. Return the beef to the pan and season with salt and freshly ground black pepper.

6. Tip into a hot serving dish and sprinkle with basil to serve.

 QUICK COOK

Beef Cannelloni
with Basil and Mozzarella

Cannelloni is a classic Italian dish, great for feeding a crowd and for preparing ahead in one dish. The filling is mince with extra mozzarella – delicious!

Serves 6

16 cannelloni pasta tubes
1 x 125g ball mozzarella, sliced
55g (2oz) Parmesan, grated

Cannelloni Filling

1 tbsp olive oil
1 onion, finely chopped
2 garlic cloves, finely grated
400g (14oz) lean minced beef
2 tbsp plain flour
300ml (½ pint) beef stock
A few drops of
  Worcestershire sauce
4 heaped tbsp tomato purée
1 tbsp freshly chopped thyme

Tomato and Basil Sauce

1 tbsp olive oil
2 onions, diced
2 garlic cloves, finely grated
2 x 400g tins chopped
  tomatoes
1 tbsp tomato purée
½ tsp sugar (optional)
Small bunch of basil,
  leaves chopped

Mary's Tips

Can be made and assembled up to 8 hours ahead.

Freezes well before final cooking.

1. Preheat the oven to 200°C/180°C Fan/Gas 6. You will need an oblong, shallow 1.8 litre (3¼ pint) ovenproof dish.

2. To make the cannelloni filling, heat the oil in a frying pan over a high heat. Add the onion and fry for a few minutes. Add the garlic and minced beef and fry until browned, breaking up with two wooden spoons as it fries. Sprinkle over the flour and stir well. Mix in the stock, Worcestershire sauce and tomato purée, then add the thyme. Cover with a lid and leave to simmer over a low heat for about 30 minutes. Set aside to cool.

3. Meanwhile, to make the tomato and basil sauce, heat the oil in a saucepan over a high heat. Add the onions and fry for 5 minutes. Add the garlic and fry for 10 seconds. Pour in the tomatoes, tomato purée, 150ml (¼ pint) water and season with salt and freshly ground black pepper. Cover and leave to simmer over a low heat for about 30 minutes. Add the sugar, if it is a little sharp. Check the seasoning and stir in the basil. Spoon a third of the tomato sauce into the base of the dish.

4. Using a teaspoon, fill each cannelloni tube with the cold mince filling. Arrange the cannelloni in a single layer in the dish. Spoon the remaining sauce on top.

5. Scatter the mozzarella and Parmesan over the top and bake in the preheated oven for about 35–40 minutes, until the pasta is soft and the cheese has browned.

6. Serve hot with a green salad.

 FREEZES WELL

Beef Cobbler with Horseradish

A rich, deeply flavoured beef stew with horseradish and a cobbler topping. Cobbler is similar to a scone dough and is a bit different to the usual potato or pastry topping.

Serves 6

3 tbsp sunflower oil

900g (2lb) braising beef, cut into 2cm (¾in) cubes

2 large onions, roughly chopped

1 tbsp light muscovado sugar

150ml (¼ pint) red wine

30g (1oz) plain flour

300ml (½ pint) cold beef stock

2 tbsp freshly chopped thyme

1 tbsp Worcestershire sauce

350g (12oz) butternut squash, peeled and cubed (prepared weight)

2–3 tbsp hot horseradish sauce

3 tbsp freshly chopped parsley

Cobbler Topping

175g (6oz) self-raising flour

75g (3oz) butter, diced

1 tsp baking powder

Egg Wash

1 large egg, beaten

2–3 tbsp milk

❄ FREEZES WELL

1. Preheat the oven to 160°C/140°C Fan/Gas 3. You will need a large, deep ovenproof casserole about 30cm (12in) wide.

2. Heat the oil in the casserole, add the beef and brown over a high heat until golden – you may need to do this in batches. Remove the meat with a slotted spoon and set aside.

3. Add the onions to the casserole and fry over a medium heat until starting to soften. Sprinkle in the light muscovado sugar and cook until starting to brown. Pour in the wine and boil over a high heat to reduce by half.

4. Measure the flour into a jug or bowl. Whisk in the cold stock until you have a smooth, lump-free liquid. Pour this into the casserole with the onions and stir well. Add the thyme and Worcestershire sauce and return the beef to the pan. Season well with salt and freshly ground black pepper, bring to the boil, cover with a lid and transfer to the preheated oven for about 1¼–1½ hours.

5. Remove the casserole from the oven and add the squash. Return to the oven for another 45 minutes, until the beef is completely tender and the squash is soft.

6. Remove from the oven and gently stir in the horseradish sauce and parsley. Check the seasoning. Increase the oven temperature to 200°C/Fan 180°C/Gas 6.

7. To make the cobbler topping, measure the flour, butter and baking powder into a bowl. Rub the butter into the flour using your fingertips until it resembles breadcrumbs. Mix the egg and milk together in a jug to make an egg wash. Stir most of this egg wash into the flour to make a soft dough, leaving a little in the jug.

Beef stew can be made up to a day ahead.

8. Roll the cobbler dough out on to a floured work surface to a round just smaller that the surface of the casserole. Carefully lift the cobbler on top of the stew, then score into 6–8 wedges. Brush the top with egg wash and bake in the oven for about 25 minutes, until the topping is golden and firm.

9. Using a bread knife, cut through the score marks of the cobbler and lift out a wedge with the stew. Serve piping hot with green vegetables.

Lamb Steaks with Roasted Vegetable and Feta Rice

Rice is such a popular dish and brown rice is something I have grown to enjoy. Buying the precooked packets makes life very easy. You can use long grain rice, or a mixture of the two, if preferred.

Serves 4

1 small aubergine, cut into small dice

2 Romano peppers, deseeded and cut into small dice

1 large red onion, roughly chopped

2 garlic cloves, finely grated

5 tbsp olive oil

4 lamb leg steaks (about 150g/5oz each)

2 x 250g packets cooked brown rice

2 tbsp sun-dried tomato paste

150g (5oz) feta cheese, crumbed

Small bunch of mint, leaves chopped

Juice of 1 lemon

Mary's Tips

Rice can be made up to 4 hours ahead and reheated to serve.

Not suitable for freezing.

1. Preheat the oven to 220°C/200°C Fan/Gas 7.

2. Put the vegetables, garlic and 3 tablespoons of the olive oil into a large roasting tin. Season well with salt and freshly ground black pepper and toss together.

3. Arrange the vegetables in a single layer and roast in the preheated oven for about 25 minutes, or until golden and soft.

4. Meanwhile, heat a large, ovenproof frying pan over a high heat. Season the lamb and drizzle with the remaining oil. Add the lamb steaks to the hot pan and quickly brown for about 1–2 minutes on each side.

5. Transfer to the preheated oven for about 3–6 minutes, until tender but still pink. Remove from the oven, place on a warm plate and cover with foil. Set aside to rest for about 5 minutes.

6. Heat the rice according to the packet instructions. Add the hot rice, sun-dried tomato paste, feta and mint to the vegetables in the roasting tin. Season and add the lemon juice. Mix well.

7. Carve the lamb steaks and serve alongside the rice and vegetables.

 PREP AHEAD

Fast-roast Rosemary Leg of Lamb

If you are very keen on mint sauce, add a little to the gravy just before serving.

Serves 6

Oil, for greasing
About 2kg (4½lb) leg
   of lamb, bonc in
2 garlic cloves, sliced
   into slivers
2 sprigs of rosemary
3 onions, each cut
   into 8 wedges
3 red peppers, deseeded and
   chopped into large pieces
3 bay leaves
150ml (¼ pint) red wine
300ml (½ pint) good beef
   or chicken stock
1 tbsp plain flour
1 tsp sun-dried tomato paste
1 tbsp redcurrant jelly

Mary's Tips

Best made and served.

Not suitable for freezing.

1. Preheat the oven to 200°C/180°C Fan/Gas 6. You will need a large, deep roasting tin with a rack.

2. Rub a little oil over the lamb, then season with sea salt and freshly ground black pepper. Make deepish holes in the meat with a small knife with a pointed blade and insert the garlic slivers into the holes. Place a few rosemary needles in each hole, too.

3. Arrange the lamb, onions and peppers on the rack. Scatter the bay leaves and any remaining rosemary sprigs around the lamb. Pour the wine and 150ml (¼ pint) of the stock into the tin. Roast the lamb in the preheated oven for about 1½ hours. Check on the lamb during the cooking time – if it is getting too brown, cover with foil. If all the liquid evaporates (this will depend on the size of your tin), add some more stock.

4. Transfer the vegetables to a serving plate and keep warm. Discard the bay leaves and rosemary sprigs. Place the lamb on a carving board, cover with foil and set aside to rest.

5. To make the gravy, place the roasting tin on the hob over a medium heat and sprinkle in the flour. Whisk the flour into the cooking juices, then pour in the remaining stock and boil for few minutes. Add the tomato paste and redcurrant jelly and mix well. Check the seasoning.

6. Carve the lamb into thinnish slices and serve with the vegetables and gravy.

 ONE POT

Friday Night Lamb Curry

A fragrant curry made with fresh tomatoes and lentils. Serve with basmati rice and poppadoms. Use leg or neck fillet for this recipe as it has a long, slow, cooking time.

Serves 6

Curry Paste
75g (3oz) pitted soft dates
75ml (3fl oz) boiling water
30g (1oz) fresh root ginger,
 peeled and grated
4 garlic cloves, finely grated
½–1 small red chilli,
 deseeded and chopped
1 tbsp each of ground
 cumin, ground coriander
 and garam masala
3 tbsp tomato purée

1kg (2lb 4oz) diced lamb leg
4 tbsp sunflower oil
3 onions, roughly chopped
500g (1lb 2oz) fresh
 tomatoes, chopped
300ml (½ pint) chicken
 or beef stock
55g (2oz) dried red lentils
Handful of freshly chopped
 coriander, to serve

Mary's Tips

*Can be made up to a day
ahead. Curry paste keeps
for 3 days in the fridge.*

Freezes well.

1. First make the curry paste. Place the dates in a small bowl, pour over the boiling water and leave to soak for 15 minutes until plump.

2. Using a slotted spoon, scoop out the dates and place them in a small food processor. Add 3 tablespoons of the soaking liquid and blend until smooth. Add the remaining ingredients and blend again until you have a thick curry paste.

3. Season the lamb with salt and freshly ground black pepper. Heat half the oil in a large frying pan over a high heat, add the lamb and brown quickly – you may need to do this in batches. Remove the lamb from the pan and set aside.

4. Add the remaining oil and the onions to the pan and fry for about 4–5 minutes. Stir in the paste and fry for 30 seconds. Add the tomatoes and stock, and bring to the boil.

5. Return the lamb to the pan, add the lentils and stir well. Cover with a lid, reduce the heat and leave to simmer for about 1½ hours.

6. Remove the lid and continue to simmer for a further 10 minutes until the lamb is tender and the sauce has reduced to a rich consistency.

7. Check the seasoning and sprinkle with coriander. Serve with rice and poppadoms.

 ONE POT

Slow-braised Lamb with Tomatoes and Borlotti Beans

Bursting with flavour, this lamb dish is a meal in itself. Lamb neck fillets need long, slow cooking to become tender and give maximum flavour and we often use them in a casserole. Borlotti beans are popular and are sometimes known as cranberry beans, due to their pink, speckled appearance. They have a creamy and slightly nutty flavour and keep their shape during long, slow cooking. If you wish to use dried beans, cook them first.

Serves 6

3 large lamb neck fillets
(about 250g/9oz each),
trimmed, kept whole

2 tbsp sunflower oil

1 large onion, thinly sliced

2 celery sticks, diced

2 garlic cloves, finely grated

1 x 400g tin chopped
tomatoes

400ml (14fl oz) chicken stock

2 tbsp tomato purée

2 tbsp freshly chopped
thyme leaves

1 x 400g tin borlotti
beans, drained

Mary's Tips

Can be made up to a day ahead and reheated all in one dish to serve. Carve the lamb just before serving.

Not suitable for freezing.

1. Preheat the oven to 160°C/140°C Fan/Gas 3.

2. Place a small, flameproof roasting tin on the hob to heat. Season the lamb and brown in the tin on all sides. Set aside.

3. Add the oil, onion and celery and fry for 5 minutes. Add the garlic and fry for 30 seconds. Stir in the tomatoes, stock, purée, thyme and beans. Bring up to the boil. Add the lamb fillets and press down into the sauce. Cover with foil and transfer to the oven for about 2 hours until tender.

4. Rest the lamb for 5 minutes, then carve into thick pieces and serve it with the braised beans and tomato sauce.

 ONE POT

Vegetable Mains

Spinach Dhal

A traditional Indian vegetarian dish, dhal (or dal) is usually made from split peas or lentils but beans and chickpeas can also be used. Intense with classic flavours, it is good served with naan, other curries or poppadoms. If using dried lentils, cook them first in water. Do not add salt until the end of cooking, as this can toughen the lentils before they are soft. You could use green lentils, which are more reasonably priced than puy lentils – but we think puy lentils have a superior flavour.

Serves 4–6

3 tbsp sunflower oil

3 large onions, finely chopped

4 garlic cloves, finely grated

2 tsp ground turmeric

1 tbsp garam masala

1 tbsp ground cumin

½ tsp hot chilli powder

1 x 400g tin chopped tomatoes

300ml (½ pint) vegetable stock

2 x 400g tins puy lentils, drained

150g (5oz) baby spinach, chopped

1 tbsp mango chutney

4 tbsp pouring double cream

Mary's Tips

Can be made up to 6 hours ahead and reheated slowly to serve.

Freezes well without the spinach or cream.

1. Heat the oil in a large saucepan over a high heat. Add the onions and fry for about 5 minutes. Add the garlic and cook for 1 minute. Stir in the spices and fry for another 2 minutes.

2. Add the tomatoes, pour in the stock and tip in the lentils, and mix well. Cover with a lid and bring up the boil. Reduce the heat and simmer for about 30 minutes, until the onions are tender.

3. Add the spinach, chutney and cream, stir and season with salt and freshly ground black pepper. Simmer until the spinach has wilted.

4. Serve hot.

 ONE POT

Warming Welsh Rarebit

An 18th-century dish, this was originally called Welsh rabbit but the name changed because of the confusion caused by assuming the recipe contained rabbit! It is more than simply cheese on toast – it is a delicious, cheesy sauce on toast that is indulgent and a real treat. Traditionally, the recipe would have included beer, but we have left this out as it is not to our taste.

Serves 4

30g (1oz) butter
200g (7oz) strong mature Cheddar, grated
2 tsp Dijon mustard
1 tbsp milk
4 slices wholemeal bread

Mary's Tips

Best made and served.

Not suitable for freezing.

1. Preheat the grill to high.

2. Melt the butter in a small saucepan over a medium heat. Add the cheese, mustard and milk and stir until the cheese has melted and the mixture has a smooth sauce consistency.

3. Meanwhile, place the bread on a baking sheet and toast under the grill on both sides.

4. Divide the cheese sauce between the slices, spooning it on to the surface and spreading it out to the edges. Put the baking sheet back under the grill for about 5 minutes, until the cheese is golden brown and bubbling.

5. Leave to cool slightly before slicing into fingers or triangles to serve.

5 5 INGREDIENTS OR FEWER

Classic Tomato and Basil Spaghetti

It is always good to have a classic tomato sauce up your sleeve. Add chilli, if you like, to give it a kick. Plum tomatoes give a deeper flavour than standard tinned tomatoes, so it's good to use them for this recipe.

Serves 6

3 tbsp olive oil
2 onions, finely diced
3 garlic cloves, finely grated
100ml (3½fl oz) white wine
2 x 400g tins plum tomatoes
2 tbsp sun-dried tomato paste
1–2 tsp caster sugar
350g (12oz) spaghetti
Small bunch of basil,
  leaves chopped
Parmesan shavings, to serve

Mary's Tips

*Sauce can be made up
to 3 days ahead.*

Sauce freezes well.

1. Place the olive oil in a shallow, lidded, frying pan over a high heat. Add the onions and cook for about 5 minutes, stirring. Lower the heat, cover with a lid and cook for about 10 minutes.

2. Add the garlic and fry for 30 seconds, then pour in the white wine and boil over the heat to reduce by half. Add the plum tomatoes, tomato paste and sugar, and season with salt and freshly ground black pepper. Cover and simmer gently for 40 minutes.

3. Remove the lid and simmer for another 5 minutes, stirring, to thicken the sauce and ensure the plum tomatoes have broken down.

4. Meanwhile, cook the spaghetti until *al dente* in boiling salted water according to the packet instructions. Drain and reserve 2 tablespoons of the pasta water.

5. Add the reserved water to the tomato sauce and stir in the chopped basil. Bring to a boil, check the seasoning and tip in the cooked spaghetti. Toss together.

6. Serve piping hot with Parmesan shavings scattered on top.

 ONE POT

Aubergine Bhuna Curry

Chicken bhuna originates from the Bengal region of India. The word bhuna is Urdu for 'fried'. It is a thick sauce of strong spices, garlic and onions. This is a delicious vegetable curry, and as lots of other curries have ground almonds in them, it is perfect for people with nut allergies.

Serves 6

4 tbsp sunflower oil

2 large onions, roughly chopped

4 garlic cloves, finely grated

½ red chilli, diced

Large piece of fresh root ginger, peeled and finely grated

1 tbsp each of ground cumin, ground coriander and curry powder

2 tsp ground turmeric

2 large aubergines, cut into large cubes

2 medium potatoes, peeled and cut in 3cm (1¼in) cubes

2 tbsp tomato purée

300g (10½oz) fresh tomatoes, roughly chopped

1 tbsp mango chutney

300ml (½ pint) vegetable stock

Mary's Tips

Can be made up to a day ahead and reheated.

Not suitable for freezing.

1. Heat the oil in a large, deep, lidded, frying pan over a high heat. Add the onions and fry for 2–3 minutes. Add the garlic, chilli and ginger and fry for a few seconds. Stir in the spices, aubergine cubes and potatoes and fry for 3–4 minutes, coating the vegetables in the spices.

2. Add the purée, tomatoes, mango chutney and stock, cover with a lid and bring up to the boil. Reduce the heat and simmer gently for about 25–30 minutes, until the potatoes are tender. Make sure you don't overcook the aubergine, as it will become mushy.

3. Season well with salt and freshly ground black pepper, and serve with rice, poppadoms and mint yoghurt, if you like.

 ONE POT

Wild Mushroom, Spinach and Roquefort Pasta Bake

An all-in-one dish, this is a family supper at its easiest. Wild mushrooms can be oyster, shiitake, morels or trompettes, so using a combination is a lovely way to give flavour and texture. Wild mushrooms bought from supermarkets are farmed by experts under controlled conditions and not sourced from the wild. It is important to pour cold water over the spinach and pasta once it is cooked, as this stops it cooking. If not, the pasta will overcook and the spinach with be brown rather than bright green.

Serves 6

225g (8oz) dried penne pasta

150g (5oz) baby spinach

30g (1oz) butter

300g (10½oz) mixed wild mushrooms, thickly sliced

400g (14oz) small button chestnut mushrooms, thickly sliced

Roquefort Sauce

30g (1oz) butter

1 onion, finely chopped

2 garlic cloves, finely grated

30g (1oz) plain flour

350ml (12fl oz) hot vegetable or chicken stock

300ml (½ pint) pouring double cream

125g (4½oz) Roquefort or other blue cheese, grated

150g (5oz) Parmesan, grated

 PREP AHEAD

1. Preheat the oven to 200°C/180°C Fan/Gas 6. You will need a 1.75-litre (3 pint) ovenproof dish.

2. Cook the penne in boiling salted water according to the packet instructions. Add the spinach 30 seconds before draining. Drain, run under cold water, then drain again and set aside.

3. Heat the butter in a large frying pan over a high heat. Add all the mushrooms and fry until lightly golden and just cooked – you may need to fry them in batches. Season with salt and freshly ground black pepper, remove the mushrooms from the pan and set aside.

4. To make the Roquefort sauce, melt the butter in the same pan over a high heat. Add the onion and garlic and fry for a few minutes. Lower the heat, cover with a lid and simmer for about 15 minutes or until soft.

5. Sprinkle in the flour and stir over the heat for 30 seconds. Gradually mix in the hot stock, stirring until thickened. Add the cream and any liquid from the mushrooms. Stir and bring to the boil. Remove from the heat and leave for 5 minutes to cool slightly.

6. Add the Roquefort and half of the Parmesan, then stir until melted and smooth. Add the cold pasta, spinach and the

Mary's Tips

Can be made and assembled up to 6 hours ahead.

Not suitable for freezing.

mushrooms. Stir well, check the seasoning, then spoon into the ovenproof dish. Sprinkle with the remaining Parmesan and bake in preheated oven for about 35 minutes, until bubbling and lightly golden on top.

7. Serve piping hot with dressed green leaves or a tomato salad.

Mixed Bean and Red Pepper Chilli

*Delicious for everyone, not just vegetarians, this healthy chilli
is bursting with flavour. Serve it with guacamole to make it
extra special, and with soured cream, too, if liked.*

Serves 6

2 tbsp olive oil

1 large onion, finely chopped

1 red pepper, deseeded
  and finely diced

2 garlic cloves, finely grated

1 tbsp each of ground cumin
  and ground coriander

1 tsp sweet smoked paprika

¼ tsp hot chilli powder

2 x 400g tins mixed salad
  beans, drained and rinsed

1 x 400g tin chopped
  tomatoes

500g (1lb 2oz) passata

300ml (½ pint)
  vegetable stock

1 tbsp tomato purée

1 tbsp mango chutney

1 × 198g tin sweetcorn,
  drained

Small bunch of coriander,
  leaves chopped

Mary's Tips

*Chilli can be made up to
8 hours ahead and reheated.*

Not suitable for freezing.

1. Heat the oil in a deep, lidded, frying pan over a high heat.
Add the onion and pepper and fry for 3–4 minutes. Add the
garlic and spices and fry for 10 seconds.

2. Stir in the beans, chopped tomatoes, passata, stock, purée
and mango chutney. Season with salt and freshly ground black
pepper. Bring up to the boil, then reduce the heat, cover with
a lid and simmer for about 40 minutes.

3. Check the seasoning and stir in the sweetcorn and coriander.

4. Serve the chilli hot with rice, some grated cheese, soured
cream and guacamole (see page 37), if liked.

 ONE POT

Spaghetti with Veggie Ragu

Just like a meat bolognese, this veggie version is a jumble of lovely vegetables in a basil and tomato sauce. Serve with spaghetti, tagliatelle or linguine. It is important to chop all the vegetables very finely, for a delicate sauce.

Serves 4–6

300g (10½oz) spaghetti
30g (1oz) Parmesan
  shavings, to serve

Veggie Ragu
2 tbsp olive oil
1 large onion, finely diced
1 celery stick, finely diced
1 red pepper, deseeded
  and finely diced
1 small courgette, finely diced
115g (4oz) button
  mushrooms, finely diced
2 large garlic cloves,
  finely grated
150ml (¼ pint) red wine
1 x 400g tin chopped
  tomatoes
2 tbsp sun-dried tomato paste
1 tsp sugar
75g (3oz) baby spinach,
  roughly chopped
2 tbsp freshly chopped
  basil leaves

1. To make the ragu sauce, heat the oil in a medium saucepan over a high heat. Add the onion, celery and red pepper and fry for a few minutes. Add the courgette, mushrooms and garlic and fry for 3–4 minutes.

2. Stir in the wine, tomatoes, tomato paste and sugar and season with salt and freshly ground black pepper. Bring up to the boil, then reduce the heat, cover with a lid and simmer for about 20 minutes, or until softened and reduced to a thick sauce.

3. Add the spinach and basil and stir until wilted. Check the seasoning.

4. Meanwhile, cook the spaghetti in boiling salted water according to the packet instructions. Drain and tip the pasta into the sauce, mixing well.

5. Serve piled into warm bowls with shavings of Parmesan.

Mary's Tips

Sauce can be made up to 6 hours ahead and reheated.

Ragu sauce freezes well.

 PREP AHEAD

Humble Pie

Hearty, warming and a real treat!

Serves 6

1 large cauliflower

2 leeks, trimmed and cut into 2cm (¾in) slices

115g (4oz) frozen petits pois

1 x 375g packet ready-rolled puff pastry

Knob of butter

200g (7oz) button mushrooms, halved

1 egg, beaten

Cheese Sauce

55g (2oz) butter

55g (2oz) plain flour

450ml (¾ pint) hot milk

2 tsp Dijon mustard

115g (4oz) mature Cheddar, coarsely grated

55g (2oz) Parmesan, coarsely grated

Mary's Tips

The pie can be made, left unglazed and kept covered in the fridge for up to 24 hours ahead.

Not suitable for freezing.

1. Preheat the oven to 200c/180c Fan/Gas 6. You will need a fairly deep 28cm (11in) diameter dish or a 3-pint dish.

2. Break the cauliflower into fairly small, even-sized florets. Some of the smaller leaves can be chopped into pieces.

3. Bring a large pan of salted water to the boil. Add the leeks and boil for 4 minutes. Add the cauliflower florets and leaves, and bring back to a boil for 3 minutes until just tender. Drain and run under cold water to stop the cooking. Drain well and set aside.

4. To make the cheese sauce, melt the butter in a large saucepan over a medium heat. Sprinkle in the flour and stir for 1 minute. Gradually add the hot milk, whisking until thickened. Stir in the mustard, Cheddar and Parmesan, and season well with salt and freshly ground black pepper. Leave to cool for 5 minutes.

5. Heat the butter over a high heat, pan fry the mushrooms for 3 minutes until golden and season with salt and pepper, set aside to cool. Add all the cold vegetables and frozen peas to the cheese sauce, stir and check the seasoning. Spoon into the pie dish.

6. Unroll the pastry and remove a 7cm (2¾in) strip from the short side and chill in the fridge. Roll out the remaining pastry to slightly bigger that the top of your pie dish. Brush beaten egg around the edge of the dish, then place the pastry on top and press down on the edges to seal. Trim any excess pastry with a sharp knife and make a small slit in the centre for the steam to escape. Brush the top with beaten egg.

 PREP AHEAD

7. Roll out the reserved strip of pastry to be a bit thinner, then roll it up tightly. Using a sharp knife, slice to make long thin strips. Unravel and dip them into the egg wash, then arrange on top of the pie, in a random pattern. Bake in the preheated oven for about 40–45 minutes, until the pastry is golden and the sauce is bubbling around the edges.

Roasted Vegetable Wellington

This is an impressive vegetarian main course with a hint of goat's cheese and delicious cheesy pastry. Hard goat's cheese can be cubed or grated, and is slightly milder than soft goat's cheese.

Serves 8

3 large onions, sliced into wedges

500g (1lb 2oz) peeled butternut squash, cubed (prepared weight)

1 red pepper, deseeded and sliced into large pieces

2 tbsp olive oil

250g (9oz) chestnut mushrooms, thickly sliced

2 garlic cloves, finely grated

150g (5oz) vegetarian hard goat's cheese, cubed

1 egg, beaten

Pastry

1 × 320g block all-butter puff pastry

1 egg, beaten

115g (3½oz) vegetarian hard goat's cheese, grated

Mary's Tips

Can be assembled up to 2 hours ahead and cooked to serve.

Not suitable for freezing.

PREP AHEAD

1. Preheat the oven to 200°C/180°C Fan/Gas 6.

2. Scatter the onions, squash and red pepper into a large roasting tin. Season with salt and freshly ground black pepper and drizzle over the oil, tossing to coat the vegetables. Roast in the preheated oven for about 20–25 minutes.

3. Add the mushrooms and garlic to the roasting tin, and stir to distribute the garlic. Drizzle with a little extra olive oil if needed. Return to the oven for about 10 minutes, until all the vegetables are tender. Set aside to cool.

4. Tip the cold vegetables into a large bowl. Add the goat's cheese, egg and more seasoning.

5. Roll out the pastry block to a 30 × 35cm (12 × 14in) rectangle. Brush the whole surface with some of the beaten egg.

6. Place the cold filling in the centre of the pastry in a log shape about 12.5 × 23cm (5 × 9in). Fold in the sides to encase the filling and roll into a neat log shape. Turn the pastry over so the seal is underneath. Chill in the fridge for 1 hour.

7. Whilst the Wellington is chilling, set the oven to 220°C/200°C Fan/Gas 7 and place a large baking sheet in the oven to heat.

8. Place the Wellington on a piece of non-stick baking paper. Brush with the remaining beaten egg and sprinkle with the grated goat's cheese. Slide onto the hot baking sheet and cook in the preheated oven for about 40 minutes until golden and crisp.

9. Cut into thick slices and serve with dressed salad leaves.

Ciabatta Tricolore

Like a pizza, this is an easy lunch to make. The tricolore are the three colours of the avocado, tomato and mozzarella, which give it a wonderful summery feel.

Serves 6

1 large ciabatta loaf
4 heaped tbsp sun-dried tomato paste
3 tbsp full-fat cream cheese
1 garlic clove, finely grated
2 tbsp freshly chopped basil, plus extra to garnish
1 large avocado, peeled and thinly sliced
4 large tomatoes, sliced
150g (5oz) mozzarella, diced
Balsamic glaze, to drizzle

Mary's Tips

Can be assembled up to 2 hours ahead. Add the avocado slices just before grilling.

Not suitable for freezing.

1. Preheat the grill to high.

2. Slice the ciabatta in half lengthways through the middle. Place the slices, cut side up, on a flat baking sheet. Toast under the grill for about 3–4 minutes, until lightly brown and crisp on the outside.

3. Mix the sun-dried tomato paste with the cream cheese, garlic and basil in a bowl. Spread this mixture on the toasted side of the bread.

4. Neatly arrange piles of tomato and avocado slices on top of the cream cheese mixture, then scatter over the diced mozzarella. Season well with salt and freshly ground black pepper and return them to the grill for about 5 minutes, or until the cheese has melted and is tinged brown.

5. Place the slices on a serving board, sprinkle with the extra basil and drizzle with the balsamic glaze. Cut each slice into three and serve at once with a green salad.

QUICK COOK

Sweet Potato and Celeriac Spiralized Linguine

You will need a spiralizer for this recipe, which is a good, inexpensive kitchen gadget to have. If you don't have a spiralizer, use a potato peeler and make ribbons. With plant-based dishes being more and more popular, a spiralizer is great for making vegetables the star of the show. A healthy and delicious veggie main, this is like a pasta dish but with no pasta! Replace one of the vegetables with courgette, if preferred.

Serves 4–6

350g (12oz) celeriac, peeled
300g (10½oz) sweet
    potato, peeled
3 large tomatoes
3 tbsp olive oil
3 tbsp sun-dried tomato paste
Bunch of basil, leaves torn
115g (4oz) feta
    cheese, crumbed

Mary's Tips

Best made and served.

Not suitable for freezing.

1. Slice the celeriac and sweet potato into long pieces and make linguine-style ribbons using a spiralizer or potato peeler.

2. Bring a pan of water to the boil. Score a cross on the base of the tomatoes and place in the boiling water for about 30 seconds. Remove from the water using a slotted spoon and transfer to a bowl of cold water. Carefully peel the skin from the tomatoes, then cut them in half and scoop out the seeds. Chop the flesh into small dice.

3. Using the same pan of water, add a good pinch of salt and bring back to the boil. Add the celeriac and sweet potato linguine and boil for 30 seconds. Drain and set aside.

4. Put the oil, diced tomatoes and sun-dried tomato paste into a large frying pan over a medium-low heat and warm through.

5. Add the celeriac and sweet potato linguine and carefully toss in the tomato mixture. Season well with salt and freshly ground black pepper, then add the basil and feta.

6. Toss again and serve at once.

 QUICK COOK

Nourish Bowls

A nourish or poke bowl is a new trend to me and I like it a lot! Made up of five elements – protein, grains, vegetables, dressing and seeds – it makes for a very healthy meal. Chia seeds are part of the mint family, and a rich source of minerals.

Serves 4

1 large sweet potato, peeled, sliced and cut into 2cm (¾in) cubes
2 tbsp olive oil
1 tsp ground cumin
2 large eggs
150g (5oz) soya beans
1 large carrot, peeled and grated
150g (5oz) cooked beetroot, peeled and diced
1 celery stick, trimmed and diced
3 spring onions, trimmed and sliced
150g (5oz) feta cheese
Small bunch of coriander, leaves chopped
115g (4oz) cooked brown rice
1 avocado, peeled and sliced
2 tbsp chia seeds

Dressing

1½ tbsp white wine vinegar
1 tbsp balsamic vinegar
8 tbsp olive oil
1 tbsp Dijon mustard
1 tbsp maple syrup

Mary's Tips

Can be assembled up to 8 hours ahead. Add avocado and dressing just before serving.

Not suitable for freezing.

1. You will need 4 small to medium bowls.

2. Preheat the oven to 220°C/200°C Fan/Gas 7 and line a baking sheet with non-stick baking paper.

3. Put the sweet potato on the prepared baking sheet and drizzle with the oil. Season with salt and freshly ground black pepper and sprinkle over the cumin. Toss to coat in the spice. Roast in the preheated oven for about 25–30 minutes, until golden brown and tender. Set aside to cool.

4. Put the eggs into a small pan of cold water. Bring up to the boil and cook for 10 minutes. Drain and run under cold water. Peel and discard the shells. Slice the eggs in half.

5. Cook the soya beans in boiling water according to the packet instructions. Drain and run under cold water.

6. Mix the carrot, beetroot, celery and spring onions together in a bowl. Season well.

7. Cube or break the feta into small pieces and mix with the coriander.

8. Combine the dressing ingredients in a jug and whisk together.

9. To assemble the bowls, arrange the sweet potato on one side of each bowl and the brown rice on the other. Add piles of the beetroot mixture, the coriander-infused feta and the soya beans. Put half an egg in each bowl and place slices of avocado on top. Sprinkle with chia seeds.

10. Pour the dressing over each bowl just before serving.

 PREP AHEAD

Super Quick Brown Rice Veg Stir-fry

A full-flavoured rice dish packed with vegetables and a hint of spice, too. Peppadew peppers are baby bell peppers bought in jars and they have a punchy flavour.

Serves 4

2 x 250g packets cooked
  brown basmati rice

2 tbsp sunflower oil

1 onion, roughly chopped

1 large carrot, peeled
  and diced

250g (9oz) brown chestnut
  mushrooms, finely diced

150g (5oz) sugar snap peas,
  sliced in half lengthways

1 tsp Chinese five spice

2 garlic cloves, finely grated

5 Peppadew peppers
  from a jar, sliced

2 tbsp soy sauce

55g (2oz) cashew nuts

Juice of ½ lemon

Mary's Tips

Best made and served.

Not suitable for freezing.

1. Heat the rice according to the packet instructions.

2. Meanwhile, heat the oil in a large frying pan over a high heat. Add the onion and carrot and fry for 3 minutes. Add the mushrooms and sugar snap peas and fry for another 3 minutes. Stir in the five spice, garlic and Peppadew peppers and fry for 30 seconds.

3. Add the cooked rice, soy, cashews and lemon juice. Season well with salt and freshly ground black pepper and toss together over the heat.

4. Serve piping hot.

 QUICK COOK

Golden Mushroom and Halloumi

Light and simple, serve this with dressed salad leaves for a lovely summery dish.

Serves 4

2 tbsp sunflower oil

4 large flat mushrooms,
stalks removed

Large knob of butter

2 garlic cloves, finely grated

4 tbsp red onion
marmalade from a jar

½ bunch of basil,
leaves chopped

250g (9oz) halloumi cheese,
cut into 4 large slices

12 cherry tomatoes

A little balsamic
glaze, to garnish

Mary's Tips

*Can be assembled up
to 30 minutes ahead.*

Not suitable for freezing.

1. Preheat the oven to 220°C/200°C Fan/Gas 7.

2. Place a frying pan over a high heat until hot. Add the oil and the mushrooms and fry for 45 seconds on each side. Add the butter and garlic and baste the mushrooms in the melted butter.

3. Transfer the mushrooms onto a baking sheet, gill-side up, and season with salt and freshly ground black pepper. Spoon a tablespoon of onion marmalade into the centre of each mushroom and sprinkle over half the basil.

4. Add the halloumi to the frying pan and brown on one side until golden. Place the halloumi browned-side up on top of the mushrooms. Put a cluster of 3 cherry tomatoes on top of each slice of cheese and season. Roast the mushroom stacks in the preheated oven for 8 minutes.

5. Remove from the oven, sprinkle with the remaining basil and drizzle with a little balsamic glaze to serve.

 QUICK COOK

Spiced Grilled Aubergine
with Tahini Dressing

Great as part of a sharing platter or served as a side dish.
The dressing would work well with roasted peppers or courgettes too.

Serves 6

3 aubergines
1 tsp sweet smoked paprika
1 tsp ground cumin
1 tsp harissa paste
1 tbsp olive oil
2 tbsp freshly chopped mint
2 tbsp freshly chopped
   parsley
½ red chilli, deseeded
   and finely chopped

Tahini Dressing
3 tbsp tahini
4 tbsp olive oil
½ garlic clove, finely grated
½ tsp ground cumin
Juice of ½ lemon

Mary's Tips

Aubergine slices can be grilled up to 2 hours ahead. Tahini dressing can be made up to a day ahead.

Not suitable for freezing.

1. Preheat the grill to high.

2. Trim the aubergines, then cut into long, thin slices, each about 1cm (½in) thick. Arrange them on a large flat baking sheet.

3. Measure the paprika, cumin, harissa and olive oil into a bowl and mix well. Brush this spiced oil over both sides of each aubergine slice. Season well with salt and freshly ground black pepper. Place the aubergine slices under the grill for about 8 minutes, then turn and grill on the other side for another 8 minutes, until brown and slightly crisp.

4. Meanwhile, mix all the dressing ingredients together in a small bowl.

5. Place the aubergine on a serving platter, scatter over the mint, parsley and chilli, and drizzle the dressing over the top before serving warm or cold.

 PREP AHEAD

Salads
and Sides

Kale and Pak Choi Stir-fry

Kale is not my favourite vegetable, but I know it is very popular so have included this recipe! You could use sliced spring greens or spinach instead, if preferred. Step up the chilli if you like it hot!

Serves 4

225g (8oz) pak choi
2 tbsp sesame seeds
1 tbsp sunflower oil
150g (5oz) young kale leaves, torn into small pieces

Sauce

2 tbsp soy sauce
1 tbsp cornflour
¼ red chilli, deseeded and diced
1 garlic clove, finely grated
2 tbsp sunflower oil
2 tsp light muscovado sugar

Mary's Tips

Cook and serve at once.
Not suitable for freezing.

1. To make the sauce, mix the ingredients together in a small bowl.

2. Cut each pak choi bulb lengthways into four.

3. Place a large frying pan over a medium heat. Add the sesame seeds and toast until golden brown. Tip the seeds on to a plate.

4. Pour the sunflower oil into the pan, set over a high heat. Add the kale and fry for a few seconds. Add 3 tablespoons of water, cover with a lid and fry for 2 minutes until just wilted.

5. Remove the lid and add the pak choi. Stir-fry for a few minutes until the kale and pak choi are just tender, but still with a little crunch.

6. Add the sauce and fry for a few seconds to heat through.

7. Spoon into a dish and sprinkle with the toasted sesame seeds to serve.

 QUICK COOK

Carrot and Beetroot Slaw with Lemon and Coriander

Fresh and bright in colour, this is quick to make and perfect for any party. Raw beetroot is delicious, and works really well in a slaw.

Serves 6–8

600g (1lb 5oz) raw beetroot, peeled

3 large carrots, peeled

4 spring onions, trimmed and finely sliced

Small bunch of coriander, leaves chopped

Balsamic Dressing

Zest and juice of 1 large lemon

6 tbsp olive oil

2 tbsp balsamic vinegar

Mary's Tips

Keeps well dressed for up to 4 hours.

Not suitable for freezing.

1. Coarsely grate the beetroot and carrot and tip into a large bowl. Stir in the spring onions and coriander. Mix and season well with salt and freshly ground black pepper.

2. Measure the dressing ingredients into a jug. Mix well, then pour over the vegetables. Toss together and serve.

QUICK COOK

Glorious Greens with Almonds and Seeds

*The most wonderful bowl of mixed green vegetables,
with seeds and nuts for extra texture.*

Serves 4–6

300g (10½oz) frozen
  petits pois
300g (10½oz) tenderstem
  broccoli, trimmed
200g (7oz) sugar snap
  peas, strings removed
Knob of butter
2 tbsp pumpkin seeds
1 tbsp sunflower seeds
30g (1oz) flaked almonds

Mary's Tips

Best made and served.

Not suitable for freezing.

1. Bring a large saucepan of salted water to the boil. Add the petits pois, return to the boil and cook for 1 minute. Add the broccoli and sugar snap peas and boil for 3 minutes. Remove from the heat, drain and tip back into the saucepan.

2. Add the butter and mix gently until melted.

3. Meanwhile, place a small non-stick frying pan over a medium heat. Add the seeds and almonds and dry fry gently until golden.

4. Tip the vegetables into a warm dish and sprinkle with the almonds and seeds to serve.

 QUICK COOK

Quinoa and Soya Bean Salad with Preserved Lemon Dressing

So healthy and quick to make, you could replace the quinoa with couscous, if preferred. It is good to used mixed quinoa, as it gives different colour and texture. Soya beans are edamame beans out of their pods and you can buy them in the salad aisle of the supermarket, or frozen. If you buy frozen, you'll need to cook them according to the packet instructions.

Serves 4–6

225g (8oz) mixed quinoa

225g (8oz) cooked soya beans

Large bunch each of mint, parsley and coriander, leaves picked

200g (7oz) feta cheese, broken into pieces

115g (4oz) gherkins, finely chopped

Dressing

1 preserved lemon, chopped

1 small garlic clove, finely grated

4 tbsp olive oil

2 tbsp white wine vinegar

Juice of 1 lemon

Mary's Tips

Can be made up to 8 hours ahead. Dress up to an hour before serving.

Not suitable for freezing.

1. Cook the quinoa according to the packet instructions.

2. Tip the quinoa into a bowl and add the soya beans, herbs, feta and gherkins. Season with salt and freshly ground black pepper and mix well.

3. Place all the dressing ingredients in a jar, seal with a lid and shake to combine.

4. Pour the dressing over the salad and mix well just before serving.

 PREP AHEAD

Mini Dauphinoise Potatoes

*These are a joy – individual moulds of dauphinoise! And they are an easy
way to serve potatoes for a special supper. Dariole moulds are little domed
metal pudding moulds which are so useful and perfect for all sorts of
dishes, including small syrup sponge puddings, pâté and panna cotta.*

Serves 8

30g (1oz) butter, melted

300ml (½ pint) pouring
double cream

1 garlic clove, finely grated

700g (1lb 9oz) medium
potatoes, peeled and cut
into very thin slices

115g (4oz) mature
Cheddar, grated

Mary's Tips

*Can be cooked up to an hour
ahead. Reheat to serve.*

Not suitable for freezing.

1. Preheat the oven to 200°C/180°C Fan/Gas 6 and grease
8 metal dariole pudding moulds with the melted butter.
Cut 8 small squares of non-stick baking paper and place
one in the base of each mould.

2. Mix the double cream and garlic together in a jug and
season with salt and freshly ground black pepper.

3. Using half the cheese, place some in the base of each of
the moulds. Arrange a slice of potato on top, then pour over
a little garlic cream. Continue to layer the potatoes and cream,
adding a little seasoning in between the layers, until finished.

4. Cover the tops of each mould with foil and seal tightly. Put
the moulds on a baking sheet (foil side up!) and bake in the
preheated oven for about 30 minutes.

5. Remove the foil and sprinkle the tops with the remaining
cheese. Bake, uncovered, for a further 15–20 minutes, until the
potatoes are cooked and the cheese is golden brown.

6. Leave in the moulds for a few minutes until any bubbling
has stopped, then slide a small palette knife around the edge
of the mould and invert on to a plate. Carefully remove the
mould and paper. Serve hot.

 PREP AHEAD

Honey-glazed Roasted Parsnips and Carrots

Two root vegetables that roast together well in one dish. It's good to cook the parsnips a little before roasting, as this keeps their shape and prevents them from shrivelling.

Serves 6

500g (1lb 2oz) large
 parsnips, peeled
3 tbsp sunflower oil
 or goose fat
500g (1lb 2oz) carrots, peeled
 and cut into batons
1 tbsp runny honey
1 tbsp freshly chopped
 flat-leaf parsley

Mary's Tips

Can be prepared and the parsnips cooked up to 6 hours ahead. Roast and serve.

Not suitable for freezing.

1. Preheat the oven to 220°C/200°C Fan/Gas 7 and put a large roasting tin in the oven to get hot.

2. Cut the parsnips in half lengthways and half again widthways. Place in a pan of boiling salted water and cook for about 5 minutes. Drain.

3. Place the oil in the hot roasting tin. Add the vegetables and turn once to coat in the oil. Season with salt and freshly ground black pepper and roast in the preheated oven for about 25–35 minutes, turning once. Five minutes before the end of the cooking time, drizzle the honey over the vegetables and return to the oven until golden brown and cooked through.

4. Sprinkle with parsley and sea salt before serving.

 PREP AHEAD

Twice-cooked Golden Roast Potatoes

A roast potato should be ultra-crispy and golden on the outside with a fluffy middle. Par-boiling them ahead and roughening them up before roasting gives a lovely crunchy outside, and semolina gives an extra crunchy edge. Cooking twice gives you time to use the oven for other things, especially if cooking a Sunday roast when oven space can be limited.

Serves 6

1.5kg (3lb 5oz) potatoes, such as King Edward or Maris Piper, peeled and cut into halves or quarters (1.25kg/2lb 12oz prepared weight)
40g (1½oz) semolina
4 tbsp goose fat or oil
3 sprigs of thyme leaves

Mary's Tips

Freezes well.

1. Preheat the oven to 220°C/200°C Fan/Gas 7 and place a large shallow roasting tin in the oven to get hot.

2. Add the potatoes to a large saucepan of cold salted water. Bring up to the boil and boil for about 5 minutes until starting to soften around the edges. Drain in a colander until completely dry, then return the potatoes to the saucepan and shake to roughen up the edges. Sprinkle in the semolina and shake again until coated.

3. Place the fat in the roasting tin and heat in the oven for about 5 minutes until smoking. Carefully tip in the potatoes and turn in the fat to coat. Scatter over the thyme and roast in the oven for about 40 minutes, turning halfway. Remove from the oven and set aside until needed. This can be done up to 12 hours ahead.

4. On the day of serving, re-roast in a hot oven for about 15–20 minutes, until golden brown and crisp.

5. Serve piping hot.

 PREP AHEAD

Sprouts with Peas and Cashew Nuts

*No Christmas table would be complete without sprouts, so this is perfect
for that time of year, but it's good enough to serve any time. We hope
mixing sprouts with peas will make them more attractive to children!*

Serves 8

500g (1lb 2oz) sprouts

500g (1lb 2oz) frozen
petits pois

Knob of butter

3 banana shallots, finely sliced

55g (2oz) salted cashew nuts

Mary's Tips

*Prepare the sprouts the day
before – put them in a polythene
bag and keep in the fridge. No
need to keep them in water.*

Not suitable for freezing.

1. Prepare the sprouts by removing the outer leaves and cutting
each one in half. Cook them in boiling salted water for 1
minute. Add the petits pois and cook for another 3–4 minutes,
depending on the size of the sprouts, until just cooked.

2. Place the butter in a large frying pan, add the shallots
and fry them over a medium heat for few minutes. Add the
sprouts, peas and cashew nuts and fry for a few more minutes,
until piping hot.

3. Season with salt and freshly ground black pepper and serve
at once.

 QUICK COOK

Spiced Red Cabbage

This completes the Christmas feast, so traditional and delicious. It is worth reducing the liquid at the end, as this gives the gloss and extra flavour.

Serves 8

1 tbsp olive oil

3 knobs of butter

1 large onion, roughly chopped

1 red dessert apple, peeled, cored and cut into 2cm (¾in) pieces

1.5kg (3lb 5oz) red cabbage, finely shredded

450ml (¾ pint) apple juice

2 bay leaves

1 cinnamon stick

Gratings of nutmeg

4 tbsp redcurrant jelly

Mary's Tips

Make completely up to a day ahead and reheat to serve.

Freeze up to a month ahead.

1. Preheat the oven to 150°C/130°C Fan/Gas 2.

2. Heat the oil and one knob of the butter in a deep ovenproof saucepan over a high heat. Add the onion, apple and cabbage and fry for about 3–4 minutes.

3. Pour in the apple juice and add the bay leaves, cinnamon, nutmeg and jelly. Season with salt and freshly ground black pepper and bring to the boil. Boil for a few minutes, then cover with a lid and transfer to the oven for about 3 hours, until completely tender.

4. Remove the cabbage using a slotted spoon to a warm serving dish.

5. Transfer the pan to the hob over a high heat and reduce the liquid until the colour has darkened and is a coating consistency. Add the remaining butter and mix well. Remove from the heat and pour over the cabbage to serve.

 FREEZES WELL

Roasted Cauliflower Salad with Grainy Mustard Dressing

Quick and so tasty, this is the perfect side salad. It is like a potato salad, which was so popular in the 80s! Any leftover cauliflower stalks can be used for soup.

Serves 4–6

1 large cauliflower, broken into small florets
2 tbsp olive oil
115g (4oz) mayonnaise
2 tbsp grainy mustard
3 tbsp freshly chopped parsley

Mary's Tips

Can be assembled up to 6 hours ahead.

Not suitable for freezing.

1. Preheat the oven to 220°C/200°C Fan/Gas 7.

2. Scatter the cauliflower florets over the base of a large roasting tin. Drizzle the oil over the florets and season well with salt and freshly ground black pepper. Roast in the preheated oven for about 15 minutes until lightly golden and just tender. Set aside to cool.

3. Measure the mayo, mustard and parsley into a bowl. Add the cold cauliflower and season well. Mix together and check the seasoning.

4. Spoon into a large dish to serve.

5 INGREDIENTS OR FEWER

Savoy Cabbage and Celeriac Stir-fry

A quick and different vegetable dish to serve alongside a roast or other meat or fish. Cabbage is a wonderful but slightly forgotten vegetable. Savoy cabbage is wrinkly around the edges, which is so attractive, but this would be delicious with pointed spring cabbage as well.

Serves 4–6

1 savoy cabbage,
   finely shredded
150g (5oz) celeriac, peeled
   and coarsely grated
Knob of butter
1 garlic clove, finely grated

Mary's Tips

The cabbage and celeriac can be boiled up to an hour ahead, drained and refreshed in cold water. Stir-fry to serve.

Not suitable for freezing.

1. Bring a pan of salted water to the boil, add the cabbage and celeriac and boil for 2 minutes. Drain.

2. Heat the butter and garlic in a large frying pan over a high heat. Add the drained cabbage and celeriac and toss in the butter.

3. Season well with sea salt and freshly ground black pepper, toss again and serve immediately.

5 INGREDIENTS
OR FEWER

Avocado Caesar Salad

A traditional Caesar salad dressing includes a raw or coddled egg, but I use mayonnaise here instead to give a creamy consistency. You could add crispy bacon and cooked chicken, if liked. Shaking the bread and oil in a bag is a top tip for getting crispy croûtons – if oil is simply poured over the bread in the frying pan, it can become soggy.

Serves 4

2 Romaine lettuces
55g (2oz) Parmesan shavings
1 x 50g can anchovy
    fillets in oil, drained
    and halved (optional)
1 large avocado, peeled
    and sliced

Sourdough Croûtons

4 thick slices day-old
    sourdough or white bread
2–4 tbsp sunflower oil

Caesar Dressing

100ml (3½fl oz) mayonnaise
Juice of ½ lemon
2 tsp Worcestershire sauce
30g (1oz) Parmesan,
    finely grated
1 garlic clove, finely grated
1 tbsp olive oil

Mary's Tips

Croûtons can be made up to a week ahead. Assemble the salad to serve.

Not suitable for freezing.

1. First make the croûtons. Stack the slices of day-old bread and cut off the crusts. Cut the bread into 1cm (½in) cubes. Place the bread in a plastic bag with the sunflower oil and some salt and freshly ground black pepper. Seal the bag and shake it well.

2. Place a large non-stick frying pan over a medium heat. When the pan is hot, add the bread cubes and cook, stirring occasionally, until they are golden all over. Remove, drain on kitchen paper to remove excess oil, and set aside to cool.

3. To make the dressing, spoon the mayonnaise into a bowl. Add the lemon juice, Worcestershire sauce, Parmesan, garlic and seasoning. Gradually add the oil, whisking all the time, until well mixed.

4. Cut the Romaine lettuce into pieces and tip into a salad bowl. Add the Parmesan shavings, croûtons, anchovy fillets, if using, and avocado.

5. Pour over the dressing and toss to combine.

 QUICK COOK

Beefsteak Tomato Salad with Balsamic Dressing

A simple tomato salad is often one of the best side dishes. Using tomatoes at their very best is a real treat. Beefsteak tomatoes are large, the size of a tennis ball, and bursting with flavour.

Serves 4–6

4 large red beefsteak
    tomatoes
4 spring onions,
    trimmed and sliced
3 tbsp freshly chopped basil

Balsamic Dressing
6 tbsp olive oil
1 tbsp Dijon mustard
2 tbsp balsamic vinegar
1 tsp caster sugar
½ garlic clove, finely grated
1 tbsp water

1. Remove the stem from the tomatoes, and slice into 0.5cm (¼in) slices. Arrange on a platter.

2. Sprinkle with the spring onions and basil, and season well with sea salt and freshly ground black pepper.

3. Mix the dressing ingredients together in a jug and whisk until smooth.

4. Pour the dressing over the salad to serve.

Mary's Tips

Dressing can be made up to a week ahead. Assemble up to an hour ahead. Dress just before serving.

Not suitable for freezing.

QUICK COOK

Garlic Summer Veg

Quick and extremely simple. Good to serve alongside chops or steaks.

Serves 4–6

2 tbsp sunflower oil
1 large onion, thinly sliced
1 red pepper, deseeded
  and sliced
30g (1oz) butter
1 garlic clove, finely grated
400g (14oz) small thin
  courgettes, sliced
  on the diagonal
Juice of ½ lemon

1. Heat the oil in a large frying pan or wok over a high heat. Add the onion and pepper and fry for about 4–5 minutes, until soft and lightly golden.

2. Add the butter and garlic and fry for 30 seconds. Add the courgettes and fry for 2 minutes, until just cooked but firm.

3. Season well with salt and freshly ground black pepper, pour over the lemon juice, spoon into a serving dish and serve at once.

Mary's Tips

Best made and served.

Not suitable for freezing.

 QUICK COOK

Swede and Carrot Purée

*Great to make ahead and it is attractive, too, with its bright orange colour.
I am generous with the pepper, as it brings out the flavour of the veg.*

Serves 6

1kg (2lb 4oz) swede,
    peeled and cut in
    2cm (¾in) chunks
500g (1lb 2oz) carrots,
    peeled and cut into
    2cm (¾in) chunks
55g (2oz) butter
½ tsp grated nutmeg

Mary's Tips

*To make ahead, spoon into a
buttered ovenproof dish and
cool. To reheat, cover with foil
and place in a hot oven.*

Freezes well.

1. Bring a large pan of salted water to the boil. Add the swede
and carrot and boil for 10 minutes or until tender.

2. Drain, tip the cubes into a processor and add the butter and
nutmeg. Season with salt and freshly ground black pepper and
whiz for a minute until smooth.

3. Serve hot.

5 5 INGREDIENTS
OR FEWER

Baking

Apple and Mincemeat Squares

This is a quick way to make a mince pie of sorts and is great when serving numbers. Adding apple to mincemeat makes it milder, and go further.

**Cuts into
9 squares**

Filling

Knob of butter

500g (1lb 2oz) Bramley
  apples, peeled,
  cored and diced

2 tbsp caster sugar

2 tbsp water

1 tbsp brandy

1 × 410g jar luxury
  mincemeat

Pastry

225g (8oz) plain flour

115g (4oz) butter, diced

30g (1oz) icing sugar

Finely grated zest
  of 1 orange

1 tbsp water

2 eggs, beaten

<u>Mary's Tips</u>

*Can be made up
to 2 days ahead.*

FREEZES WELL

1. You will need an 18cm (7in) square toffee tin.

2. To make the filling, melt the butter in a large frying pan over a medium heat. Add the apple, sugar and water. Stir, then cover with a lid and cook for about 3–4 minutes, until the apple is soft but not mushy. Transfer to a bowl and set aside to cool.

3. Add the brandy and mincemeat to the apple and chill in the fridge while the pastry is made.

4. Measure the flour and butter into a food processor and whiz until it resembles breadcrumbs. Add the icing sugar, orange zest, water and half the egg and whiz again until the pastry comes together. Knead into a ball, then roll out to a thin rectangle, double the length of the tin but the same width.

5. Line the base and sizes of the tin with the pastry, aligning one edge with the rim of the tin and leaving the remaining pastry overhanging. Spoon the filling into the tin. Brush the edges of the pastry with some of the remaining egg, then fold the overhanging pastry over to make the top. Press down lightly around the edges and trim the excess pastry. Using a small knife, gently score the pastry to give a pretty finish. Brush the top with beaten egg and chill in the fridge for about 30 minutes, if you have time.

6. Preheat the oven to 200°C/180°C Fan/Gas 6 and place a heavy baking sheet in the oven to heat.

7. Place the pie on the hot baking sheet and bake in the preheated oven for about 35–45 minutes, or until the pastry is golden and crisp. Leave to cool before slicing into squares or fingers to serve, with brandy butter if liked.

Bara Brith

This is a classic Welsh teabread, so easy to make as it is an all-in-one cake and keeps well. Literally translated it means 'speckled bread', presumably due to its appearance.

Makes 1 × 900g (2lb) loaf

300ml (½ pint) strong
   tea of your choice
90g (3½oz) sultanas
90g (3½oz) raisins
90g (3½oz) dried cranberries
90g (3½oz) currants
Butter, for greasing
½ tsp ground mixed spice
225g (8oz) light
   muscovado sugar
275g (10oz) self-raising flour
1 egg, beaten

Mary's Tips

Can be made up to 3 days ahead.

1. Make the tea in a teapot, or use the remains of leftover tea, then pour it into a large heatproof bowl. Add all the fruits and stir to coat. Cover and leave for minimum of 6 hours or overnight to allow the fruit to absorb the tea and plump up.

2. Preheat the oven to 160°C/140°C Fan/Gas 3. Grease and line a 900g (2lb) loaf tin with non-stick baking paper.

3. Add the spice, sugar, flour and egg to the fruits and mix well. Spoon into the prepared tin and level the surface. Bake in the preheated oven for about 1½ hours, until well risen and firm to the touch. Insert a skewer into the middle of the cake; if it comes out clean then the loaf is ready. Leave in the tin to cool for 10 minutes before turning out onto a wire rack to cool completely.

4. Slice into fairly thick slices and spread with butter to serve. Add some red jam as well, if liked!

 FREEZES WELL

Very Berry Christmas Fruit Cake

An easy fruit cake which works well plain or would be lovely for an occasion if iced and decorated. Use whisky or dark rum instead of brandy if preferred.

Cuts into about 20 slices

225g (8oz) ready-to-eat apricots, finely chopped
450g (1lb) raisins
200g (7oz) dried cranberries
150g (5oz) dried blueberries
225g (8oz) currants
125ml (4fl oz) brandy
225g (8oz) butter, softened, plus extra for greasing
250g (9oz) light muscovado sugar
5 large eggs
225g (8oz) plain flour
2 tsp ground mixed spice

Mary's Tips

Can be made up to 4 days ahead.

1. Place all the fruits and brandy in a large bowl. Stir to coat the fruit, then cover and leave for at least 6 hours or overnight to allow the fruits to absorb the brandy and plump up.

2. Preheat the oven to 140°C/120°C Fan/Gas 2.

3. Grease and line a 20cm (8in) square cake tin with non-stick baking paper.

4. Measure the butter, sugar, eggs, flour and spice into a large bowl. Beat together using an electric hand whisk or wooden spoon until combined. Stir in the soaked fruits.

5. Spoon into the prepared tin and level the top. Bake in the preheated oven for about 4½ hours until lightly golden. Test if the cake is cooked by inserting a skewer into the centre; if it comes out clean then the cake is ready.

6. Leave to cool in the tin for 10 minutes, then remove and cool completely on a wire rack.

 FREEZES WELL

Bûche de Noël

*French for 'yule log', and the perfect Christmas treat, this bake has
a whipped cream and brandy filling. If preferred, add sweetened
chestnut purée to the brandy cream, instead of the hazelnuts.*

Serves 8–10

Roulade
Butter, for greasing
180g (6oz) plain chocolate,
  broken into pieces
6 eggs, separated
175g (6oz) caster sugar
10g (¼oz) cocoa powder,
  sifted, plus extra to dust
Icing sugar, to dust

Filling
2 tbsp brandy
150ml (¼ pint) pouring
  double cream, lightly
  whipped to soft peaks
55g (2oz) roasted hazelnuts,
  finely chopped

Ganache
300ml (½ pint) pouring
  double cream, whipped
360g (12oz) plain chocolate,
  broken into pieces

PREP AHEAD

1. Preheat the oven to 180°C/160°C Fan/Gas 4. Grease a
33 x 23cm (13 x 9in) Swiss roll tin and line with non-stick
baking paper.

2. To melt the chocolate, place the chocolate pieces for the
roulade in a heatproof bowl over a pan of hot water until
melted, making sure the base of the bowl is not touching
the water. Allow to cool slightly until warm but still runny.

3. Whisk the egg whites in a large mixing bowl on high
speed until stiff but not dry.

4. In a separate large bowl, whisk the sugar and egg yolks
until light, thick and creamy. Add the melted chocolate and
gently stir until blended. Stir two large spoonfuls of the egg
whites into the chocolate mixture, mix gently, then fold in
the remaining egg whites. Finally, fold in the sifted cocoa.

5. Turn the mixture into the prepared tin and gently level
the surface. Bake in the preheated oven for about 25 minutes,
until risen and firm in the centre. Remove from the oven,
leave in the tin (expect the roulade to dip and crack a little)
and set aside until cold.

6. Meanwhile, make the ganache. Measure the cream into a
pan and place over a medium heat until hot. Remove from the
heat, add the chocolate pieces and stir until melted. Set aside
to cool, then chill in the fridge to become firm and very stiff.

7. Put a large piece of baking paper onto a work surface and
dust with cocoa powder. Tip the roulade tin upside down onto
the paper. Remove the tin and paper, then brush the surface of
the roulade with brandy.

Can be made and assembled up to 8 hours ahead. Keep in the fridge and lift out 2 hours before serving.

Not suitable for freezing.

Do not use a high cocoa content chocolate; use around a 40% cocoa solids.

8. Make a 2cm (¾in) mark along one long edge of the roulade using a knife (be careful not to cut through). Spread the whipped cream over the roulade, then scatter the hazelnuts over the cream. Using the paper, roll the roulade where it is scored to make a tight roll. Slice a quarter of the roulade at one end on an angle. Place the large piece of roulade on a serving plate and attach the quarter to look like a branch.

9. Spoon the ganache topping into a large piping bag fitted with a star nozzle. Pipe rows of ganache icing over the roulade to create a bark effect. Sprinkle with icing sugar and place a sprig of holly on top to serve.

Mary's Tips

Can be made, assembled and piped up to 6 hours ahead. The cakes can be made a day ahead, ready to ice on the day.

Freezes well iced.

Use around 40% cocoa solids chocolate.

FREEZES WELL

Elderflower and Lemon Traybake

Light and fresh, this will be enjoyed by all. Edible flowers make a wonderful decoration and can be bought easily in markets and specialist shops. My favourites are the bright blue borage flowers from the summer herb or tiny pansies, when in season.

Cuts into 16 squares

Traybake
Butter, for greasing
4 large eggs
225g (8oz) caster sugar
225g (8oz) self-raising flour
225g (8oz) baking spread, straight from the fridge
1 tsp baking powder
Finely grated zest of 1 lemon
2 tbsp elderflower cordial

Lemon Icing
200g (7oz) icing sugar
3–4 tbsp fresh lemon juice
16 borage leaves or edible flowers

1. Preheat the oven to 180°C/160°C Fan/Gas 4. Grease and line a 30 x 23cm (12 x 9in) traybake tin with non-stick baking paper.

2. Measure all the traybake ingredients into a large mixing bowl. Whisk using an electric hand whisk until light and fluffy.

3. Spoon into the tin and level the surface. Bake in the preheated oven for about 30–35 minutes, until well risen and lightly golden. Leave to cool in the tin on a wire rack, then turn out and remove the baking paper.

4. To make the icing, sift the icing sugar into a bowl. Add the lemon juice and mix until the consistency of smooth glacé icing.

5. Spread the icing over the cooled cake and decorate with edible flowers to serve.

Mary's Tips

Can be made up to a day ahead. It is best iced and decorated on the day.

Freezes well un-iced.

FREEZES WELL

Grown-u

Sometimes it can be
one which is not com
is the one! A grown
iced. If serving as

Serves 30 or mor

For One Traybake
(you will need two
for this recipe)
30g (1oz) cocoa powder
5 tbsp boiling water
225g (8oz) caster sugar
225g (8oz) baking spread
   straight from the fridge
275g (10oz) self-raising f
1 tsp baking powder
4 large eggs
1 tbsp milk

Ganache Icing
450ml (¾ pint) pouring
   double cream
450g (1lb) plain chocola
   broken into pieces

Filling
4 tbsp cream liqueur
   (such as Baileys,
   Kahlúa or Amarula)
300ml (½ pint) pouring
   double cream, whippe
   to soft peaks

Decoration
175g (6oz) Maltesers
8 chocolate truffles,
   roughly chopped

Madeleines

A delicious French treat. The traditional way to eat them is with a cup of tea, and dip if you like! The specialist tins are worth investing in as these are so pretty. If you only have one tin, the mixture will keep until the first tin is baked, then grease and flour the tin again and repeat until all the mixture has been used up.

Makes 24–32

150g (5oz) butter, melted, plus extra for greasing
150g (5oz) self-raising flour, plus extra for dusting
3 eggs
150g (5oz) caster sugar
½ tsp baking powder
Finely grated zest of 1 lemon
Icing sugar, to dust

Mary's Tips

Best made and eaten on the day of baking.

Not suitable for freezing.

1. Preheat the oven to 220°C/Fan 200°C/Gas 7. Grease two 12-hole Madeleine trays, dust with flour and shake off any excess.

2. Measure the eggs and sugar into a large bowl and mix using an electric whisk until pale and thick, and the mixture leaves a prominent trail when the whisk is lifted.

3. Sift half the flour into the mixture, add the baking powder and lemon zest and very gently fold the mixture until incorporated. Be careful not to mix too much or you will lose air. Pour in half the melted butter around the edge of the bowl and carefully fold in. Repeat the process with the remaining flour and butter.

4. Spoon the mixture into the prepared moulds so that it falls just below the rim. Bake in the preheated oven for about 8–10 minutes, until well risen, golden and springy to the touch.

5. Using a small palette knife, gently tip the cakes from the tin and cool on a wire rack.

6. Dust with icing sugar to serve.

 QUICK COOK

Walnut and Coffee Sandwich Cake

The name may seem familiar, but this is a walnut cake with coffee icing rather than the traditional coffee and walnut cake, which is a coffee cake with a walnut decoration. The sponge has a nutty, speckled look and texture. The icing should be smooth and well flavoured with coffee. Taste it once you have made it and add more dissolved coffee, if liked.

Serves 8

Walnut Cake

Butter, for greasing
225g (8oz) self-raising flour
1 tsp baking powder
100g (3½oz) walnuts,
  very finely chopped
225g (8oz) baking spread,
  straight from the fridge
225g (8oz) caster sugar
4 large eggs
1 tbsp very strong coffee

Coffee Icing

115g (4oz) butter, softened
2 tbsp very strong coffee
225g (8oz) icing sugar, sifted

Mary's Tips

Cakes can be made up to a day ahead. Best to ice on the day of serving.

Cakes freeze well un-iced.

1. Preheat the oven to 180°C/160°C Fan/Gas 4. Grease and base line 2 x 20cm (8in) sponge sandwich tins with non-stick baking paper.

2. Measure all the walnut cake ingredients into a large mixing bowl. Mix using an electric whisk for about 2 minutes, until light and fluffy.

3. Divide the mixture evenly between the tins and level the surfaces. Bake in the preheated oven for about 25–30 minutes, until pale golden and well risen. Leave to cool in the tins for 10 minutes, then carefully turn out, remove the paper and cool on wire racks.

4. To make the icing, mix the butter, coffee and half the icing sugar together in a large bowl using an electric whisk. Add the remaining icing sugar and mix again.

5. To assemble the cake, put one sponge upside down on a plate. Spread half the icing on top. Put the second cake on top and decorate with the remaining icing. Use the back of a teaspoon to decorate the surface with a scalloped spiral pattern.

 FREEZES WELL

Red Velvet Sandwich Cake

An impressive but easy cake. Use a professional food colouring paste, if you can; a natural liquid colouring won't work and may turn the sponge green.

Serves 8

Butter, for greasing
250g (9oz) plain flour
1 tbsp cocoa powder
2 tsp baking powder
1 tsp bicarbonate of soda
250g (9oz) light
   muscovado sugar
200ml (⅓ pint) buttermilk
150ml (¼ pint) sunflower oil
2 tsp vanilla extract
1 tbsp red food colouring
   gel or about ¼ tsp food
   colouring paste
2 large eggs
8 white chocolate truffle
   balls, to decorate

Buttercream Icing
250g (9oz) butter, softened
2 tsp vanilla extract
300g (10½oz) icing sugar
250g (9oz) full-fat
   mascarpone cheese

1. Preheat the oven to 180°C/160°C Fan/Gas 4. Grease and line the bases of 2 × 20cm (8in) sponge sandwich tins with non-stick baking paper.

2. Measure the flour, cocoa powder, baking powder, bicarbonate of soda and sugar into a bowl and mix well.

3. Mix the buttermilk, oil, vanilla, food colouring and 100ml (3½fl oz) water in a jug. Add the eggs and whisk until smooth. Pour the wet ingredients into the dry ingredients and whisk until combined. The mixture should be bright red; it will get a little darker as it cooks. If it's not as vivid as you'd like, add a touch more colouring.

4. Divide the mixture evenly between the two prepared tins and level the surfaces. Bake in the preheated oven for about 25–30 minutes, or until well risen and shrinking away from the sides of the tins. Cool in the tins for 10 minutes, then turn out, peel off the paper and leave to cool completely on a wire rack.

5. To make the buttercream icing, place the soft butter and vanilla extract in a large bowl and sift in half the icing sugar. Mix with an electric whisk until smooth. Sift in the remaining icing sugar and mix again. Add the mascarpone to the bowl and gently stir with a spatula until smooth (don't beat with a whisk as it may split). Put a fluted nozzle in a piping bag and spoon about 150g (5oz) of the buttercream into the bag.

6. To assemble the cake, sit one of the sponges on a cake plate and spread a third of the buttercream over the cake, then sit the other cake on top. Ice the cake by first spreading a thin layer of icing – a crumb coat – over the whole cake before chilling for 30 minutes. Then pile the remaining icing from the bowl

 FREEZES WELL

around the edges before starting to create lines up the sides. Using a small palette knife, make wide lines up the sides and swirl the top. Pipe a rope design around the edge of the top of the cake and decorate with the 8 chocolate truffles to finish.

Ginger Treacle Butterfly Cupcakes

Bursting with ginger and lots of rich icing, these cupcakes will be loved by all.

Makes 12

115g (4oz) baking spread, straight from the fridge

75g (3oz) caster sugar

115g (4oz) black treacle

150g (5oz) self-raising flour

1 tsp baking powder

½ tsp ground mixed spice

½ tsp ground allspice

½ tsp ground ginger

2 eggs

2 tbsp milk

7 bulbs of stem ginger from a jar, 3 bulbs finely chopped and 4 bulbs very finely sliced into strips

Ginger Buttercream

115g (4oz) butter, softened

2 tbsp ginger syrup, from the stem ginger jar

225g (8oz) icing sugar, plus extra to dust

Mary's Tips

Best made on the day but can be iced up to 6 hours ahead.

Freeze well un-iced.

1. Preheat the oven to 180°C/160°C Fan/Gas 4. Line a 12-hole muffin tin with cupcake cases.

2. Measure the cake ingredients except the stem ginger into a large bowl. Mix using an electric whisk until light and fluffy. Stir in the 3 bulbs of finely chopped stem ginger.

3. Spoon the mixture into the prepared tin and bake in the preheated oven for about 20–25 minutes, until well risen. Leave to cool on a wire rack.

4. To make the buttercream, measure the butter, ginger syrup and half the icing sugar into a bowl. Mix using an electric whisk until fluffy. Add the remaining icing sugar and mix again. Spoon the buttercream into a piping bag fitted with a fluted nozzle.

5. Using a small sharp knife, cut a shallow round circle from the centre of each cake. Slice each circle in half to make butterfly wings. Pipe some buttercream into each hole and pile more on top. Arrange the butterfly wings in the icing, then sprinkle the cakes with the sliced stem ginger strips and dust each one with icing sugar.

 PREP AHEAD

Chocolate Chip Oat Cookies

These cookies have a lovely crisp edge and squidgy middle. Watch them carefully as they cook, as they are dark in appearance so can catch easily. There are many different varieties of porridge oats available to buy, we use the traditional small – not jumbo – oats.

Makes 24

125g (4½oz) butter, softened
150g (5oz) light
   muscovado sugar
1 large egg
½ tsp vanilla extract
150g (5oz) plain flour
75g (3oz) traditional
   porridge oats
100g (3½oz) dark
   chocolate chips

Mary's Tips

Can be made up to 2 days ahead.

Freezes well.

1. Preheat the oven 180°C/160°C Fan/Gas 4. Line two baking sheets with non-stick baking paper.

2. Measure the butter and sugar into a mixing bowl. Mix with an electric whisk until light and fluffy and pale in colour. Add the egg, vanilla, flour and oats and whisk again until just mixed. Stir in the chocolate chips with a spatula.

3. Shape into 24 even-sized balls and place half of the balls spaced apart on each baking sheet. Press the top down slightly to squash each one a little flatter. Bake in the preheated oven for about 12–15 minutes, until golden brown all over. Transfer to a wire rack to cool. They will crack and crinkle and that's part of the charm.

 QUICK COOK

Old-fashioned Flapjacks with Apricots

The easiest treat and great to make ahead. Omit the apricots if you're not keen, the flapjacks will be just as delicious. If overcooked the flapjacks can become too hard; they are nicer to eat when they are a little gooier.

Cuts into 16 squares

225g (8oz) butter
225g (8oz) demerara sugar
75g (3oz) golden syrup
275g (10oz) traditional porridge oats
8 ready-to-eat dried apricots, snipped into small pieces

Mary's Tips

Can be made up to 4 days ahead.

Freezes well.

1. Preheat the oven to 160°C/140°C Fan/Gas 3. Line a 23cm (9in) square tin with non-stick baking paper.

2. Measure the butter, demerara sugar and golden syrup into a saucepan. Slowly melt over a low heat until the sugar has dissolved.

3. Remove from the heat, stir in the oats and apricots and mix well.

4. Turn the mixture into the prepared tin and press flat using the back of a spoon. Bake in the preheated oven for about 30–35 minutes, until evenly pale golden brown. Remove from the oven and leave to cool in the tin for 10 minutes.

5. Score the flapjack into 16 squares using a small sharp knife and leave to finish cooling in the tin.

 5 INGREDIENTS OR FEWER

Spiced Squash and Walnut Loaf

Don't panic, this is delicious! I know it sounds a bit odd, but think of carrot cake, courgette cake and pumpkin pie – we often use vegetables in cakes and squash works really well in this spiced loaf.

Makes 1 x 900g (2lb) loaf

Butter, for greasing
175g (6oz) coarsely grated butternut squash (prepared weight)
2 large eggs
125ml (4fl oz) sunflower oil
175g (6oz) caster sugar
90g (3½oz) plain flour
75g (3oz) buckwheat flour
½ tsp baking powder
1 tsp bicarbonate of soda
2 tsp ground cinnamon
½ tsp ground mixed spice
90g (3½oz) raisins
75g (3oz) walnuts, roughly chopped

Mary's Tips

Can be made 2 days ahead.

1. Preheat the oven to 180°C/160°C Fan/Gas 4. Grease and line 1 x 900g (2lb) loaf tin with a strip of non-stick baking paper.

2. Tip the grated squash into a large bowl and add the remaining ingredients, except the raisins and walnuts. Mix using an electric whisk until well incorporated, then stir in the raisins and walnuts.

3. Spoon into the prepared loaf tin and bake for about 1 hour – 1 hour 10 minutes until well risen and golden brown. Leave to cool for 10 minutes in the tin, then turn out and cool on a wire rack.

4. Cut into slices and serve with butter.

 FREEZES WELL

Cold
Desserts

Passion Fruit Flummery

Many moons ago I made lemon flummery, which was so popular and easy to make. It's similar to ice cream, so keep it in the freezer in small pots or ramekins, then you'll always have a pudding to hand for last-minute guests. It's best to use passion fruit when they are wrinkly, as these produce the most juice.

Makes 8–10

300ml (½ pint) pouring
   double cream
600ml (1 pint) full-fat milk
325g (11½oz) caster sugar
5 large passion fruit
Juice of 1 large lemon

Mary's Tips

Freeze up to a month ahead.

1. You will need a shallow plastic or similar container, and 8–10 freezer-proof pots or ramekins.

2. Measure the double cream into a large bowl. Whisk until soft peaks. Slowly pour in the milk, whisking until smooth. Add the sugar and whisk again.

3. Slice the passion fruit in half and scoop out the flesh. Set aside the flesh from one of the passion fruit for decoration. Push the remaining flesh through a sieve into a bowl. Discard the seeds.

4. Pour the passion fruit juice into the cream mixture. Add the lemon juice and stir well (the mixture will thicken slightly). Pour into the shallow container, cover with a lid and freeze for 8 hours or overnight.

5. When the flummery is frozen, tip out of the container onto a board and carefully cut into large pieces using a sharp knife. Put the pieces in a food processor and blend to break up the ice crystals to make a thick slush consistency. Spoon the flummery slush into the little freezer-proof pots or ramekins and level the tops. Cover each pot with foil and refreeze for 4 hours until completely frozen.

6. Before serving, remove the ramekins from the freezer for about 10 minutes to soften slightly, and drizzle some of the reserved passion fruit flesh on top.

5 5 INGREDIENTS
OR FEWER

Chocolate Perfection

Rich, indulgent and very naughty. A real treat of a pudding. This is impressive, too, with the white and dark chocolate layers and the sharp coulis on the side. Buy 100% Belgian white chocolate, as we find this the best for melting.

Serves 8–10

2 x 280g tubs full-
fat cream cheese

300ml (½ pint) pouring
double cream

200g (7oz) white chocolate,
broken into pieces

200g (7oz) dark chocolate,
broken into pieces

150g (5oz) digestive biscuits

55g (2oz) butter, plus
extra for greasing

Raspberry Coulis

300g (10½oz) raspberries

30g (1oz) icing sugar

1. Lightly grease and line a 900g (2lb) loaf tin with non-stick baking paper.

2. Remove the cream cheese and double cream from the fridge 30 minutes before making the pudding.

3. Place the white chocolate pieces in a heatproof bowl and the dark chocolate pieces in another. Place both bowls over pans of hot water, making sure the base of the bowl is not touching the water. Heat them gently, stirring until melted. Take special care with the white chocolate; allow it to get just warm and melted then take the bowl off the pan. The dark chocolate will take longer. Set aside.

4. Put the cream cheese into a large bowl and whisk until smooth using an electric whisk. Add the cream to the cream cheese and whisk until a smooth, firm peak consistency.

5. Divide the cream cheese mixture equally between the two bowls of melted chocolate. Whisk each one again using an electric whisk until well incorporated.

6. Spoon the white chocolate cream cheese mixture into the base on the loaf tin and spread out to make an even layer. Place the dark chocolate cream cheese mixture on top and spread out evenly. Be careful not to mix the two layers.

7. Crush the biscuits to fine crumbs, then melt the butter and add to the biscuits. Mix together, then spoon on top of the terrine and press down firmly to make a layer of biscuits (when the pudding is turned out, the biscuit will be the base). Cover with cling film or eco wrap and chill in the fridge for 2 hours.

 PREP AHEAD

Mary's Tips

Be careful not to overheat the chocolate; if it goes beyond lukewarm, it will not set once cooled and may split.

Can be made up to 2 days ahead.

Make sure to use white chocolate with 36% cocoa solids.

Freezes well.

8. Meanwhile, make the coulis. Reserve 10 raspberries for decoration and place the remainder into a jug. Add the icing sugar and blend using an electric hand blender until smooth. Pour the coulis through a sieve and discard the seeds.

9. Turn the terrine upside down onto a long plate. Remove the paper and arrange the 10 raspberries in a neat line on top. Cut into thick slices and serve with the coulis.

Quick Limoncello Ice Cream

A real cheat – no raw eggs and no ice cream mixer needed.
Condensed milk is sweetened milk in a tin.

Serves 6

600ml (1 pint) pouring
double cream

1 x 397g can full-fat
condensed milk

Zest of 4 lemons and
juice of 2 lemons

6 tbsp limoncello, plus
extra to serve

Mary's Tips

Keep in the freezer for
up to 3 months.

1. Whisk the double cream until lightly whipped. Stir in the condensed milk. Add the lemon zest and juice, and the limoncello and whisk again until thick and smooth.

2. Pour into a plastic container and freeze for 6 hours or overnight until frozen.

3. Scoop into balls to serve, and pour an extra limoncello shot over the top, if liked!

5 5 INGREDIENTS
OR FEWER

Super Quick Raspberry Parfait

Who doesn't like puddings that you can make ahead with no stress? Adding some of the raspberry purée to the mousse gives a lovely strong flavour.

Makes 6 small glasses

225g (8oz) raspberries
6 tbsp icing sugar
4 tbsp cassis liqueur
200g (7oz) full-fat
   mascarpone cheese
150ml (¼ pint) pouring
   double cream
Juice of ½ lemon

Mary's Tips

Can be made up to 8 hours ahead.
Not suitable for freezing.

1. Reserve 6 raspberries to decorate and place the remaining fruit in a food processor. Add 3 tablespoons of the icing sugar and all the cassis. Blend to a purée, then pour through a sieve. Discard the seeds.

2. Measure the mascarpone into a mixing bowl. Gently mix with an electric whisk to soften, then pour in the double cream, add the remaining icing sugar and whisk again. Add the lemon juice and half the raspberry purée and fold together until well incorporated. Be careful to mix and fold gently in order to keep a smooth cream.

3. Divide the mixture between 6 small glasses. Spoon the remaining raspberry coulis on top and garnish with a fresh raspberry to serve.

 QUICK COOK

Mascarpone Ice Cream with Bitter Chocolate Sauce

Classic vanilla ice cream with a rich creaminess from the mascarpone.

Serves 6

Mascarpone Ice Cream

1 x 250g tub of full-fat
mascarpone cheese

175ml (6fl oz) pouring
double cream

2 tsp vanilla extract

4 eggs, separated

175g (6oz) caster sugar

Chocolate Sauce

30g (1oz) butter

75g (3oz) golden syrup

6 tbsp water

1 tsp vanilla extract

30g (1oz) cocoa powder

55g (2oz) dark chocolate,
broken into pieces

Mary's Tips

*Ice cream can be frozen for up to
2 months. Chocolate sauce can
be made up to 3 days ahead.*

1. To make the ice cream, scoop the mascarpone into a large bowl and mix gently using an electric whisk to loosen and remove any lumps. Add the double cream and vanilla and whisk slowly until soft peaks, being careful not to overbeat.

2. Place the egg whites in another large bowl. Whisk with an electric whisk until stiff and cloud-like. Gradually add the caster sugar, a teaspoon at a time, until you have a thick, glossy meringue mixture.

3. Add a heaped tablespoon of meringue to the mascarpone cream mixture and stir to loosen. Carefully fold the loosened cream into the remaining meringue.

4. Beat the eggs yolks in a small bowl, then fold them into the mascarpone meringue and mix well.

5. Spoon the ice cream into a container and freeze overnight.

6. To make the chocolate sauce, measure all the ingredients except the dark chocolate into a small saucepan. Heat gently over a low heat until the butter has melted. Remove from the heat, add the pieces of chocolate and stir until melted and smooth. Do not boil as the sauce will lose its shine.

7. Remove the ice cream from the freezer about 10 minutes before serving. Scoop into bowls and serve with the warm bitter chocolate sauce.

 PREP AHEAD

Lemon and Mango Brûlée Top

A quick and easy pudding with a brûlée topping. Similar to the classic crème brûlée but a bit of a cheat. If you can't find a whole ripe mango, you could use the pre-packed mango in tubs.

Makes 8–10

350g (12oz) ripe mango, diced

200ml (⅓ pint) pouring double cream

1 x 397g can full-fat condensed milk

Juice of 3 lemons

Juice of 1 small orange

175g (6oz) demerara sugar

Mary's Tips

Not suitable for freezing.

Mango custard can be made up to a day ahead. Brûlée can be made an hour ahead – keep the puddings out of the fridge once the brûlée has been made.

1. You will need 8–10 ramekins or heatproof pots.

2. Put the mango pieces into a food processor and blend until completely smooth. With the motor still running, pour in the cream and condensed milk. Whiz again.

3. Remove the bowl from the mixer, use a spatula to stir in the lemon and orange juices, and the mixture will thicken.

4. Spoon into pots or ramekins and chill in the fridge for 6 hours or overnight.

5. When ready to serve, divide the sugar between the ramekins, sprinkling it on top. Use a blowtorch or slide under a hot grill to melt the sugar until a golden, crisp brûlée topping forms.

 FOR A CROWD

Key Lime Tranche

A classic American dessert, this is similar to a cheesecake but made with condensed milk. Such an easy, quick pudding that is sweet and sharp from the limes. This version is made in a rectangular tranche tin, which gives a different presentation, but the recipe would also fit in a 23cm (9in) round, deep, loose-bottomed flan tin.

Serves 6

115g (4oz) full-fat
 cream cheese
1 × 397g tin full-fat
 condensed milk
Finely grated zest and
 juice of 4 limes
200ml (⅓ pint) pouring
 double cream

Biscuit Base
115g (4oz) digestive biscuits
55g (2oz) butter
1 tsp demerara sugar

Mary's Tips

Can be made a day ahead.

Not suitable for freezing.

1. First make the base. Crush the biscuits to fine crumbs, then melt the butter and add to the biscuits. Add the sugar and mix well.

2. Spoon the biscuit into the base of a 36 x 12.5 x 2.5cm (14 x 5 x 1in) rectangular, loose-bottomed fluted tin and press down firmly using the back of a spoon. Place in the fridge to chill for at least 30 minutes.

3. To make the filling, measure the cream cheese into a bowl and mix until smooth using an electric mixer. Add the condensed milk and the zest of 2 limes and whisk lightly. Add the juice of all 4 limes and continue to whisk until the mixture has thickened.

4. Pour the filling into the tin and level the surface. Chill in the fridge for 2 hours until firm.

5. Lightly whip the cream to soft peaks. Spread over the lime mixture and lightly swirl the top.

6. Sprinkle with the remaining lime zest to serve.

 PREP AHEAD

Strawberry and Cream Ripple Pavlova

Meringues and pavlovas can seem a little daunting when you haven't made them before. In fact, follow a few foolproof rules and they will become a firm favourite. Pavlova starts off as a meringue, but vinegar and cornflour are added, which ensures it has a gooey middle after baking, and is pavlova's secret.

Serves 6

3 large egg whites
175g (6oz) caster sugar
1 tsp cornflour
1 tsp white wine vinegar
450g (1lb) strawberries
300ml (½ pint) pouring
   double cream
Icing sugar, to dust

Mary's Tips

Pavlova can be made up to a month ahead.

Freezes well but is easily damaged

1. Preheat the oven to 160°C/140°C Fan/Gas 3. Line a baking sheet with non-stick baking paper.

2. Place the egg whites in a large bowl. Whisk using an electric whisk on full speed until stiff but not dry. With the whisk still running on full speed, gradually add the caster sugar, a teaspoon at a time, until shiny and glossy and the meringue holds its shape in peaks.

3. Mix the cornflour and vinegar together in a small bowl. Stir into the meringue.

4. Spoon the meringue on to the baking sheet and, using the back of a spoon, spread out to make a rough circle measuring about 23cm (9in). Hollow the meringue slightly in the centre and raise it around the sides. Bake in the preheated oven for about 1 hour, until firm to the touch. Turn off the oven and leave the meringue inside for another hour. Remove from the oven and set aside.

5. To make the filling, remove the stalks from half of the strawberries and cut the fruit into pieces. Whiz in a food processor until smooth. Cut the remaining strawberries in half, leaving a few with stalks on for decoration.

6. Whip the cream until soft peaks, then fold half the strawberry coulis into the cream to give a rippled effect.

7. Spoon the strawberry cream into the centre of the pavlova. Scatter the remaining strawberries over the cream and drizzle the remaining coulis over the top and sides. Dust with icing sugar just before serving.

 PREP AHEAD

Oranges with Boozy Orange Cream

Orange segments with Grand Marnier syrup and served with the boozy cream below.

Serves 4

8 large oranges

200g (7oz) caster sugar

4 tbsp orange liqueur,
    such as Grand Marnier
    or Cointreau

Boozy Orange Cream

300ml (½ pint) pouring
    double cream

30g (1oz) icing sugar

Finely grated zest of 1 orange

Grand Marnier or
    Cointreau, to taste

Mary's Tips

*Cream can be made up to
2 days ahead. Oranges can be
assembled up to 8 hours ahead.*

Not for freezing.

1. Peel the oranges and remove all the white pith. Slice into discs about 0.5cm (¼in) thick. Set aside.

2. Place the sugar and 8 tablespoons of water in a stainless steel pan over a medium heat and stir until the sugar has dissolved. Boil for about 1 minute, then add the orange liqueur and set aside to cool.

3. To make the boozy cream, whip the cream with the icing sugar to form soft peaks. Fold in the orange zest and some orange liqueur to your taste – 1 tablespoon is good, 2 tablespoons even better and 3 tablespoons – wow! (You can slice the orange that is left and add it to the other orange slices, if liked.)

4. Arrange the orange slices in a lovely glass dish. If you have any excess juice, add it to the orange syrup. Pour the syrup over the oranges and serve with the boozy cream on the side.

5 INGREDIENTS
OR FEWER

Celebration Trifle

This is a lovely traditional recipe, which is always popular with the family. Rather than making a custard and worrying that it won't set, we have suggested a cheat's version here, which always gives excellent results.

Serves 6–8

1 × 400g (14oz) can pears in light syrup
8 trifle sponges
6 tbsp strawberry jam
100ml (3½fl oz) medium dry sherry
115g (4oz) maraschino cherries, drained and halved
About 10 amaretti biscuits
300ml (½ pint) pouring double cream
1 × 400g (14oz) packet or can ready-made custard

Mary's Tips

Better made a day ahead.

Not suitable for freezing.

1. You will need a straight sided glass trifle dish – ideally 10cm (4in) deep and 20cm (8in) wide.

2. Drain the pears, reserving the syrup. Cut the fruit into small pieces.

3. Split the trifle sponges in half and sandwich them together with strawberry jam. Slice 6 of the sponge sandwiches in half along the longer length.

4. Measure the sherry into a jug and make up to 150ml (¼ pint) with the reserved pear juice. (If you don't wish to have sherry in your trifle, then use all the pear juice.)

5. Arrange the trifle sponges around the edge of the dish, pushing them into the sides so the jam is visible through the glass. You will have two layers on top of each other. Put any leftover sponge sandwiches in the base of the dish, and push down to fill any gaps.

6. Scatter the pear and cherries over the sponge fingers in the base, then arrange the amaretti biscuits on top. Pour the pear juice and sherry over the biscuits and press down firmly so all the sponges are soaked in the juice and the top is level.

7. Whip half the cream until fairly stiff, then stir into the custard. Spread the custard cream mixture over the biscuits and level the top. Chill the trifle in the fridge for 30 minutes.

8. Lightly whip the remaining cream and spread over the top. Ripple the surface with a palette knife and chill until ready to serve.

9. Serve chilled.

 PREP AHEAD

Sunset Fruit Platter

This is all about presentation and is not a recipe, as such. The variety of fruits look so attractive served this way – for breakfast, brunch, dessert or any party.

Serves 8–10

1 small pineapple
225g (8oz) strawberries, halved
300g (10½oz) blueberries
1 just-ripe mango, peeled and diced
300g (10½oz) green grapes
225g (8oz) raspberries

Mary's Tips

Can be arranged up to 2 hours ahead.

Not suitable for freezing.

1. Place the pineapple on a chopping board. Slice the top off, keeping the leaves intact, and place the top of the leaves in the centre of a large circular plate or wooden board so it looks like a palm tree.

2. With the pineapple standing upright, slice into 6 wedges. Using a small knife, remove the core and run your knife between the flesh and skin. Slice the flesh into pieces and rearrange back in the skin shell, in its original shape, so you have 6 pineapple wedge shells with cut pineapple pieces inside. Arrange the wedges in a star shape around the pineapple 'tree' in the centre of the platter.

3. Arrange the strawberries in one of the gaps between two of the wedges. Continue to fill the gaps with the remaining fruits to give a wheel of colour.

 PREP AHEAD

St Clements Creams

A simple and quick dessert, that can be made ahead, too.

Makes 6

3 oranges, segmented
300ml (½ pint) pouring
    double cream
75g (3oz) caster sugar
Finely grated zest and
    juice of 2 lemons
Finely grated zest
    of ½ orange

Mary's Tips

*Can be made up to
8 hours ahead.*

Not suitable for freezing.

1. Divide half the orange segments between the base of 6 little glass pots.

2. Pour the cream into a saucepan and place over a low heat. Add the sugar, lemon zest and orange zest and heat until just before boiling, stirring continuously. Remove from the heat and set aside for a few minutes.

3. Add the juice from both lemons to the cream and stir until it thickens slightly.

4. Spoon the cream into the glasses on top of the orange segments and place them in the fridge to set overnight.

5. Remove from the fridge and decorate the top with the remaining orange segments to serve.

 5 INGREDIENTS OR FEWER

Hot Puddings

Apricot Portuguese Tarts

Such a favourite around the world and particularly in London where there are dedicated shops to the Portuguese tart. It is a worldwide treasure – pastel de nata!

Makes 10

1 x 320g packet ready-rolled all-butter puff pastry

½ x 400g tin apricots, drained and sliced

15g (½oz) demerara sugar

About 3 tbsp apricot jam, melted, to glaze

Custard

250ml (9fl oz) milk

100ml (3½fl oz) pouring double cream

1 tsp vanilla extract

1 large egg and 2 egg yolks

115g (4oz) caster sugar

4 level tsp cornflour

Mary's Tips

Can be made up to a day ahead, but best fresh on the day.

Freeze well but much better made fresh.

1. You will need a 12-hole deep muffin tin and a 10cm (4in) round cutter.

2. To make the custard, add the milk, cream and vanilla to a saucepan. Place over a medium heat until hand hot. Meanwhile, break the whole egg into a heatproof bowl, add the egg yolks, sugar and cornflour and whisk by hand until combined. Pour in the hot milk and cream and whisk again until smooth.

3. Pour the custard back into the saucepan. Place over a medium heat and whisk to a thick custard consistency. Be careful not to overheat. Spoon the custard into a bowl and cover with a piece of cling film. Set aside to become cold.

4. Unroll the pastry and cut it in half lengthways to make two strips. Sit the strips on top of each other, press down, and then cut the pastry in half widthways. Take one piece and roll it thinly to create a large piece of pastry big enough to cut 5 10cm (4in) discs from. Using a 10cm (4in) cutter, cut 5 discs out of the pastry. Repeat this process with the other piece, producing 10 round discs in total. Put the rounds in the muffin tin, press down firmly and up the sides of the tin. Prick the bases with a fork.

5. Spoon the cold custard into the pastry cases and top with the apricot slices. Chill in the fridge for 30 minutes, if you have time. Preheat the oven to 200°C/180°C Fan/Gas 6.

6. Sprinkle the tarts with the demerara sugar and bake in the preheated oven for about 25–30 minutes, until the pastry is golden and the custard is set. Remove from the oven and cool slightly.

7. Brush the melted jam over the tops of the tarts to serve.

 PREP AHEAD

Red Fruit and Almond Puddings

A perfect way to serve summer fruits, such as raspberries, blackcurrants, redcurrants and blackberries. Or you could use apples in the autumn instead.

Serves 6

300g (10½oz) frozen
   red fruits, defrosted
55g (2oz) caster sugar
1 tbsp cornflour
1 ripe pear, peeled and diced
Icing sugar, to dust

Sponge Topping

1 egg
75g (3oz) caster sugar
75g (3oz) self-raising flour
75g (3oz) baking spread,
   straight from the fridge
½ tsp almond extract
55g (2oz) flaked almonds

Mary's Tips

Best made on the day.
Not suitable for freezing.

1. Preheat the oven to 200°C/180°C Fan/Gas 6. You will need 6 x 150ml (¼ pint/size 1) ramekins or ovenproof dishes.

2. Put the defrosted red fruits, caster sugar, cornflour and pear into a bowl and mix together. Divide the mixture between the ramekins.

3. Measure all the sponge ingredients, except the flaked almonds, into a mixing bowl. Mix using an electric hand whisk for 2 minutes. Divide the sponge mixture between the ramekins and spread out on top of the fruits. Sprinkle with flaked almonds and place on a baking sheet. Bake in the preheated oven for 20–25 minutes, until well risen and lightly golden.

4. Dust with icing sugar and serve with cream.

 QUICK COOK

Traditional Syrup and Lemon Steamed Pudding

*An old-fashioned syrup pudding. The lemon is strong
and punchy so tastes fresh and light.*

Serves 6

Butter, for greasing
115g (4oz) golden syrup
125g (4½oz) baking spread,
   straight from the fridge
125g (4½oz) caster sugar
125g (4½oz) self-raising flour
2 large eggs
Finely grated zest of 4
   medium lemons

To serve
115g (4oz) golden syrup
Juice of 2 lemons

Mary's Tips

Freezes well cooked.

*Can be made up to 4 hours
ahead and reheated.*

1. Lightly butter the inside of a 900g (2lb) pudding basin
or Pyrex bowl. Place a small square of non-stick baking paper
into the base.

2. Pour the syrup for the pudding into the base of the basin.

3. Measure the baking spread, sugar, flour, eggs and lemon
zest into a bowl. Mix together using an electric whisk for
2 minutes. Spoon the mixture on top of the syrup.

4. To make a lid for the basin, cut a circle of non-stick baking
paper the same size as the top of the basin. Break off a large
square of foil about 4cm (1½in) larger than the surface of the
basin and make a pleat in the middle of the square. Place the
non-stick paper on top of the pudding, and the foil on top of
the paper. Seal around the edges tightly with string.

5. Put a metal jam jar lid into the base of a large saucepan and
sit the pudding basin on top. Fill the pan with boiling water to
halfway up the sides of the basin. Cover the saucepan with a
lid and bring up to the boil, then reduce the heat and simmer
for about 1½ hours until the sponge is well risen.

6. Turn upside down onto a plate and carefully remove the
basin and paper.

7. To serve, warm the syrup and lemon juice in a saucepan
and pour over the pudding.

 FREEZES WELL

Apple Crumble

Just a classic and the best – my ultimate favourite crumble. Although,
plum and rhubarb are up there as some of the best, too!

Serves 6

1.5kg (3lb 5oz) cooking
  apples, peeled, cored
  and roughly chopped
30g (1oz) butter
175g (6oz) light
  muscovado sugar

Crumble Topping

175g (6oz) plain flour
115g (4oz) butter,
  cut into cubes
55g (2oz) demerara sugar,
  plus a little extra to sprinkle

Mary's Tips

Can be assembled up to 6 hours
ahead. Best cooked to serve.

Freezes well assembled
and uncooked.

1. Preheat the oven to 200°C/180°C Fan/Gas 6. You will need a 25cm (10in) round shallow ovenproof pie dish.

2. Place the apples in a wide-based pan, add 2 tablespoons of water and the butter and cook over a gentle heat for about 6 minutes, until tender, stirring regularly. Remove from the heat, stir in the sugar and set aside to cool.

3. To make the crumble topping, measure the ingredients into a large bowl and rub together, using your fingertips, until the mixture looks like breadcrumbs.

4. Spoon the cold apple into the pie dish and level the surface. Sprinkle an even layer of crumble topping over the apple, then sprinkle over a little extra demerara sugar.

5. Cook in the preheated oven for 20 minutes. Lower the temperature to 180°C/160°C Fan/Gas 4 and cook for a further 20 minutes until golden and bubbling.

6. Serve hot with cream, custard, ice cream or crème fraîche!

 FREEZES WELL

Maple and Orange Pudding

This is a baked sponge with spices, orange and maple sauce.

Serves 4–6

75g (3oz) butter, softened

125g (4½oz) light
   muscovado sugar

2 eggs

175g (6oz) self-raising flour

1 tsp bicarbonate of soda

2 tbsp maple syrup

1 tsp vanilla extract

1 tsp each of mixed spice,
   ground cinnamon
   and ground ginger

Zest of 1 orange

125ml (4fl oz) milk

Maple Sauce

115g (4oz) butter

115g (4oz) light
   muscovado sugar

200ml (⅓ pint) pouring
   double cream

2 tbsp maple syrup

Mary's Tips

*Pudding can be made up to 4
hours ahead. Reheat gently and
pour the sauce over to serve.
Sauce can be made up to 2 days
ahead and reheated to serve.*

Freezes well without the sauce.

1. Preheat the oven to 180°C/160°C Fan/Gas 4. Grease a 1.75 litre (3 pint) shallow ovenproof dish.

2. To make the pudding, measure the butter and sugar into a bowl. Mix with an electric whisk until light and fluffy. Add the eggs, flour, bicarbonate of soda, maple syrup, vanilla, spices and orange zest and some of the milk. Whisk together. Slowly pour in the remaining milk to make a thick batter.

3. Pour into the prepared dish and bake in the preheated oven for about 35 minutes, until well risen and firm in the centre. Set aside to cool for 5 minutes.

4. Meanwhile, measure the sauce ingredients into a saucepan and heat until boiling, stirring all of the time.

5. Pour half of the sauce over the pudding and serve the remaining sauce alongside. Serve hot with custard, cream or ice cream.

 FREEZES WELL

Express Apple and Pear Open Pie

This is so impressive but very quick! A delicious cheat.

Serves 6

200g (7oz) Bramley apples, peeled, cored and roughly diced (prepared weight)

2 ripe pears, peeled, cored and roughly diced

4 heaped tbsp lemon curd

1 x 500g block ready-made puff pastry

1 egg, beaten

30g (1oz) demerara sugar

Icing sugar, for sprinkling

Mary's Tips

Can be assembled up to 3 hours ahead.

Not suitable for freezing.

1. Preheat the oven to 220°C/200°C Fan/Gas 7. Place a baking sheet into the oven to heat.

2. Measure the diced apples and pears into a bowl. Add the lemon curd and mix well to coat the fruit.

3. Roll out the pastry on a floured work surface to a circle and trim to a diameter of about 33cm (13in). Lift the pastry onto a sheet of baking paper.

4. Tip the apple and pear mixture into the centre of the pastry. Spread out slightly, leaving a 7.5cm (3in) border around the edge. Brush the edge of the pastry with the beaten egg, then fold the pastry over and twist to make a border. Push it together to make sides (a bit like the edge of a Cornish pasty). Brush the sides with more beaten egg, then sprinkle the demerara sugar all over the fruit and edges of the pastry. Lift the baking paper onto the hot baking sheet and bake in the preheated oven for about 35–40 minutes until golden and crisp.

5. Sprinkle with icing sugar to serve.

 QUICK COOK

Rum Baked Bananas

*A great dish for all the family – with or without the rum, children
will enjoy it! Serve with shop-bought vanilla ice cream or make the
Limoncello or Mascarpone Ice Cream on pages 241 and 245.*

Serves 6

30g (1oz) butter, softened,
  plus extra for greasing
6 just-ripe bananas, peeled
  and cut in half lengthways
2 tbsp fresh lemon juice
40g (1½oz) light
  muscovado sugar
3 tbsp dark rum

Mary's Tips

Best made and served.

Not suitable for freezing.

1. Preheat the oven to 200°C/180°C Fan/Gas 6 and butter
a shallow ovenproof dish that will fit the bananas neatly in
a single layer.

2. Arrange the bananas cut-side up snugly in the dish. Dot
with the butter, then sprinkle over the lemon juice and sugar.
Cover the dish in foil and bake in the preheated oven for
about 15 minutes.

3. Remove the foil, pour the rum around the edges (be careful
not to knock the sugar off the bananas) and return to the oven
for a final 5 minutes. The bananas should be glazed and soft.

4. Serve warm with ice cream.

 5 INGREDIENTS
OR FEWER

Hot Chocolate Pudding
with White Chocolate Cream

A delicious but very rich pudding that is incredibly quick to make.

Serves 4–6

115g (4oz) butter, softened,
   plus extra for greasing
175g (6oz) light
   muscovado sugar
2 large eggs
175g (6oz) self-raising flour
55g (2oz) cocoa
   powder, sifted
1 tsp bicarbonate of soda
1 tsp baking powder
3 tbsp golden syrup
275ml (9½fl oz) milk
150g (5oz) dark
   chocolate, melted

White Chocolate Cream

300ml (½ pint) pouring
   double cream
200g (7oz) white chocolate,
   broken into pieces
1 tsp vanilla extract

Mary's Tips

*Make the pudding a day ahead
and warm through before
serving. Gently reheat the sauce
in a pan over a low heat.*

*Cooked pudding would
freeze well.*

1. Preheat the oven to 180°C/160°C Fan/Gas 4 and butter a 1.75 litre (3 pint) ovenproof dish.

2. Measure the softened butter, sugar, eggs, flour, cocoa, bicarb, baking powder and golden syrup into a large bowl. Mix using an electric whisk for about 1 minute. Slowly pour in the milk, whisking until smooth. Whisk in the melted chocolate.

3. Pour into the prepared dish and level the surface. Bake in the preheated oven for about 35 minutes, until well risen and springy in the centre.

4. Meanwhile, make the white chocolate cream. Heat the cream in a saucepan over a medium heat until hand hot. Remove from the heat and stir in the white chocolate and vanilla until melted.

5. Pour the white chocolate cream over the chocolate pudding to serve.

 FREEZES WELL

Conversion Chart

Weights

Metric	Imperial
5g	⅛ oz
10g	¼ oz
15g	½ oz
20g	¾ oz
30g	1 oz
35g	1¼ oz
40g	1½ oz
55g	2 oz
60g	2¼ oz
65g	2½ oz
75g	3 oz
90g	3½ oz
115g	4 oz
125g	4½ oz
150g	5 oz
175g	6 oz
200g	7 oz
225g	8 oz
250g	9 oz
275g	10 oz
300g	10½ oz
325g	11½ oz
350g	12 oz
375g	13 oz
400g	14 oz
425g	15 oz
450g	1 lb
500g	1 lb 2 oz

Metric	Imperial
550g	1¼ lb
600g	1 lb 5 oz
650g	1 lb 7 oz
675g	1½ lb
700g	1 lb 9 oz
750g	1 lb 10 oz
800g	1¾ lb
850g	1 lb 14 oz
900g	2 lb
1.3kg	3 lb
1.8kg	4 lb
2.25kg	5 lb

Oven Temperatures

°C	Fan °C	°F	Gas Mark
120	100	250	½
140	120	275	1
150	130	300	2
160	140	325	3
180	160	350	4
190	170	375	5
200	180	400	6
220	200	425	7
230	210	450	8
240	220	475	9

Volume

Metric	Imperial
30ml	1 fl oz
50ml	2 fl oz
75ml	2½ fl oz
85ml	3 fl oz
100ml	3½ fl oz
125ml	4 fl oz
150ml	5 fl oz (¼ pint)
175ml	6 fl oz
200ml	7 fl oz (⅓ pint)
225ml	8 fl oz
240ml	8½ fl oz
250ml	9 fl oz
275ml	9½ fl oz
300ml	10 fl oz (½ pint)
350ml	12 fl oz
400ml	14 fl oz
450ml	15 fl oz (¾ pint)
500ml	18 fl oz
600ml	20 fl oz (1 pint)
700ml	1¼ pints
900ml	1½ pints
1 litre	1¾ pints
1.2 litres	2 pints
1.25 litres	2¼ pints
1.5 litres	2½ pints
1.75 litres	3 pints
2 litres	3½ pints
2.25 litres	4 pints
2.5 litres	4½ pints
2.75 litres	5 pints
3.4 litres	6 pints
3.9 litres	7 pints
4.5 litres	8 pints (1 gallon)

Measurements

Metric	Imperial
5mm	¼ in
1cm	½ in
1.5cm	5/8 in
2cm	¾ in
2.5cm	1 in
3cm	1¼ in
4cm	1½ in
5cm	2 in
6.5cm	2½ in
7cm	2¾ in
7.5cm	3 in
9cm	3½ in
10cm	4 in
11cm	4½ in
12.5cm	5 in
15cm	6 in
16cm	6½ in
18cm	7 in
20cm	8 in
23cm	9 in
25cm	10 in
28cm	11 in
30cm	12 in
33cm	13 in
35cm	13¾ in
36cm	14 in
40cm	15¼ in
46cm	18 in

Thank Yous

Let me just start by saying we have one big happy team, that hasn't changed over the years – we are like a family, I enjoy every working day and welcome them with open arms. It starts with coffee, tea and chat which has to be curtailed as we need to work! So my thank yous go to:

Lucy Young

- Without doubt the boss, after 33 years. Runs the ship and nothing gets past her that isn't the best.
- Luce is also in charge of laughter and fun!

Lucinda McCord

- Has been in the fold for 23 years working here, at home with Luce and me. Best home economist in the business.
- This book has been perfect with its Easy theme, as she is supermum of two children and that is the pattern she follows cooking at home!

BBC Books at Ebury Press

- Lizzy Gray, our expert publisher, and editor Phoebe Lindsley set the high standards.
- Jo Roberts Miller, our wonderful enthusiastic project editor, and a great cook too.
- Abi Hartshorne, our creative designer.

The Recipe Shoot

- Recipes double tested by Isla Murray. Lisa Harrison, our home economist on the photography shoot; they are top of the home ec tree!
- Laura Edwards for the beautiful photos, one for each recipe, and Tabitha Hawkins for the props.
- Nicky Johnston for the cover and portrait photos, he's brilliant and doesn't hang about!

Glam Squad

- Jo Penford – hair and make up extraordinaire, she is the best and has the great skill of doing my hair so that it doesn't get blown on an outside filming shoot!
- Tess Wright, super stylist, smartens me up and keeps me warm for cold filming days!

Guardian Agents

- Caroline Wood and Michele Topham at FBA, our Literary Agent, and Joanna Kaye and Theia Nankivell at KBJ Management; we couldn't wish for a more caring and dynamic team. Thank you. Thank you.

- And to our readers, the most amazing support, this is for you.

Mary Berry